Table of Contents

Table of Contents

Comprehension: "The Princess and the Pea"

Fairy tales are short stories written for children involving magical characters.

Directions: Read the story. Then answer the questions.

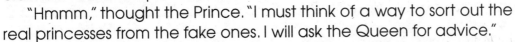

Once there was a prince who wanted to get married. The catch was, he had to marry a *real* princess. The Prince knew that real princesses were few and far between. When they heard he was looking for a bride, many young women came to the palace. All claimed to be real princesses.

"Hmmm," thought the Prince. "I must think of a way to sort out the real princesses from the fake ones. I will ask the Queen for advice."

Luckily, since he was a prince, the Queen was also his mother. So of course she had her son's best interests at heart. "A real princess is very delicate," said the Queen. "She must sleep on a mattress as soft as a cloud. If there is even a small lump, she will not be able to sleep."

"Why not?" asked the Prince. He was a nice man but not as smart as his mother.

"Because she is so delicate!" said the Queen impatiently. "Let's figure out a way to test her. Better still, let me figure out a test. You go down and pick a girl to try out my plan."

The Prince went down to the lobby of the castle. A very pretty but humble-looking girl caught his eye. He brought her back to his mother, who welcomed her.

"Please be our guest at the castle tonight," said the Queen. "Tomorrow we will talk with you about whether you are a real princess."

The pretty but humble girl was shown to her room. In it was a pile of five mattresses, all fluffy and clean. "A princess is delicate," said the Queen. "Sweet dreams!"

The girl climbed to the top of the pile and laid down, but she could not sleep. She tossed and turned and was quite cross the next morning.

"I found this under the fourth mattress when I got up this morning," she said. She handed a small green pea to the Queen. "No wonder I couldn't sleep!"

The Queen clapped her hands. The Prince looked confused. "A real princess is delicate. If this pea I put under the mattress kept you awake, you are definitely a princess."

"Of course I am," said the Princess. "Now may I please take a nap?"

1. Why does the Prince worry about finding a bride? _Because he can't tell which is the the real one of his own._

2. According to the Queen, how can the Prince tell who is a real princess? _By putting a lump under the bed._

3. Who hides something under the girl's mattress? _The Queen._

Name: _____

Comprehension: "The Princess and the Pea"

Directions: Review the story "The Princess and the Pea." Then answer the questions.

1. Why does the Prince need a test to see who is a real princess?

So he can get married.

_____

2. Why does the Princess have trouble sleeping? Because there is a pea under her bed.

3. In this story, the Queen puts a small pea under a pile of mattresses to see if the girl is delicate. What else could be done to test a princess for delicacy? A lego peace, a peace of wood, a wristwatch, a nailclip.

_____

The story does not tell whether or not the Prince and Princess get married and live happily ever after, only that the Princess wants to take a nap.

Directions: Write a new ending to the story.

4. What do you think happens after the Princess wakes up?

She takes the pea out and puts it under the queen'sesmattress tostestfor her decacy."Now it's your turn." the princess cackles.

_____

_____

_____

_____

Name: _____

Comprehension: "The Frog Prince"

Directions: Read the story "The Frog Prince." Then answer the questions.

Once upon a time, there lived a beautiful princess who liked to play alone in the woods. One day, as she was playing with her golden ball, it rolled into a lake. The water was so deep she could not see the ball. The Princess was very sad. She cried out, "I would give anything to have my golden ball back!"

Suddenly, a large ugly frog popped out of the water. "Anything?" he croaked. The Princess looked at him with distaste. "Yes," she said, "I would give anything."

"I will get your golden ball," said the frog. "In return, you must take me back to the castle. You must let me live with you and eat from your golden plate."

"Whatever you want," said the Princess. She thought the frog was very ugly, but she wanted her golden ball.

The frog dove down and brought the ball to the Princess. She put the frog in her pocket and took him home. "He is ugly," the Princess said. "But a promise is a promise. And a princess always keeps her word."

The Princess changed her clothes and forgot all about the frog. That evening, she heard a tapping at her door. She ran to the door to open it and a handsome prince stepped in.

"Who are you?" asked the Princess, already half in love.

"I am the prince you rescued at the lake," said the handsome Prince. "I was turned into a frog one hundred years ago today by a wicked lady. Because they always keep their promises, only a beautiful princess could break the spell. You are a little forgetful, but you did keep your word!"

Can you guess what happened next? Of course, they were married and lived happily ever after.

1. What does the frog ask the Princess to promise? _That she must let_
him live with her and let him off her golden plate.

2. Where does the Princess put the frog when she leaves the lake? _She puts_
him in her pocket.

3. Why could only a princess break the spell? _Because princesesily_
always keep their promises.

Comprehension: "The Frog Prince"

Directions: Review the story "The Frog Prince." Then answer the questions.

1. What does the Princess lose in the lake? _a golden ball_

2. How does she get it back? _She gets it back by having the frog do it for her._

3. How does the frog turn back into a prince? _By the princeses promise of letting him live in her palace._

4. What phrases are used to begin and end this story? _"Once upon a time" and "they lived happilly ever after."_

5. Are these words used frequently to begin and end fairy tales? _yes_

There is more than one version of most fairy tales. In another version of this story, the Princess has to kiss the frog in order for him to change back into a prince.

Directions: Write your answers.

6. What do you think would happen in a story where the Princess kisses the frog, but he remains a frog?

She regrets what she did and feels disgustid.

7. What kinds of problems would a princess have with a bossy frog in the castle? Brainstorm ideas and write them here.

work, mad, unhappy, disgusted, regretful.

8. Rewrite the ending to "The Frog Prince" so that the frog remains a frog and does not turn into a handsome prince.

And they lived unhappilly ever after.

Creative Writing: Your Own Fairy Tale

All stories need a **beginning**, a **middle** and an **ending**. The beginning introduces the characters and the setting. It tells what problem needs to be solved.

The middle of a story shows the action—what the characters try to do to solve the problem.

The ending of a story tells how the characters solved the problem and what happened at the end.

Directions: Write your own fairy tale.

Beginning _____

_____

_____

_____

_____

_____

Middle _____

_____

_____

_____

_____

_____

_____

Ending _____

_____

_____

_____

Review

Directions: Think of fairy tales you know from books or videos, like "Cinderella," "Snow White," "Sleeping Beauty," "Rapunzel" and "Beauty and the Beast." Then answer the questions.

1. What are some common elements in all fairy tales? _____

_____

2. How do fairy tales usually begin? _____

_____

3. How do fairy tales usually end? _____

_____

Directions: Locate and read several different versions of the same fairy tale. For example: "Cinderella," "Princess Furball," "Cinderlad" and "Yah Shen." Then answer the questions.

4. How are the stories alike? _____

_____

_____

_____

5. How are they different? _____

_____

_____

_____

6. Which story is best developed by the author? _____

7. Which story did you like best? Why? _____

_____

_____

Review

Most of us have read many fairy tales and have seen them in movies. Fairy tales have a certain style and format they usually follow.

Directions: Use another sheet of paper to write another fairy tale. Use the following questions to help you brainstorm ideas.

1. What is the name of the kingdom? _____

2. What is the size of the kingdom, its climate, trees, plants, animals, etc.? _____

_____

_____

3. What kind of magic happens there? _____

_____

4. Who are the characters?
   Good guys   Bad guys

_____   _____

_____   _____

5. What does each character look like? _____

_____

6. What kind of spell is cast on a particular character and why? _____

_____

_____

_____

7. What happens to the good characters and the bad characters in the end?

_____

_____

Name: _____

Following Directions: Early Native Americans

Directions: Read about the early Native Americans. Then work the puzzle.

There were about 300 Native American tribes in North America when the first white settlers came to New England in the 1500s. These Native Americans loved and respected the earth. They hunted buffalo on the plains. They fished in the clear rivers. They planted corn and beans on the rich land. They gathered roots and herbs. Before the white settlers drove them out, the Native Americans were masters of the land and all its riches.

The Native Americans grew crops, hunted for food, made clothing and built their homes from what they found on the land in the area where they lived. That is why each tribe of Native Americans was different. Some Native Americans lived in special tents called tepees. Some lived in adobe pueblos. Some lived in simple huts called hogans.

Across:

2. Native American homes made of adobe
3. Native Americans hunted this animal.
4. Tents some Native Americans lived in

Down:

1. Huts some Native Americans lived in
4. There were this many hundred tribes of Native Americans when settlers came.
5. All the tribes loved the _____.

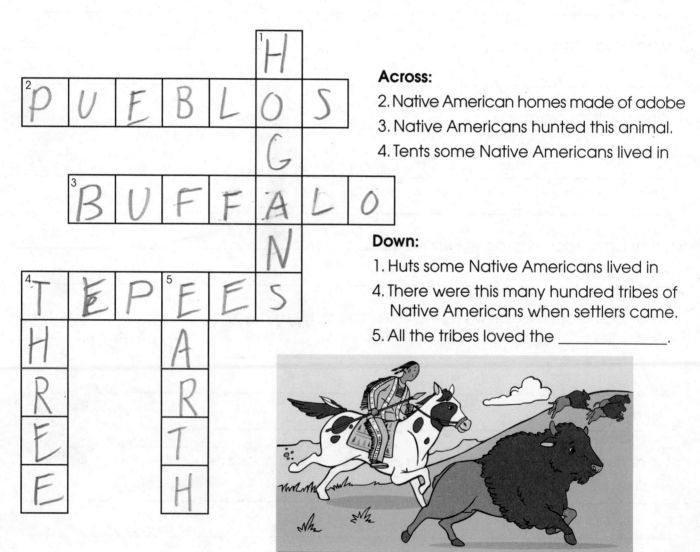

Comprehension: The Pueblo People

Directions: Read about the Pueblo people. Then answer the questions.

Long ago, Native Americans occupied all the land that is now Arizona, New Mexico, Utah and parts of California and Colorado. Twenty-five different tribes lived in this southwestern area. Several of the tribes lived in villages called pueblos. The Hopi (hope-ee) Indians lived in pueblos. So did the Zuñi (zoo-nee) and the Laguna (lah-goon-nah). These and other tribes who lived in villages were called the "Pueblo people."

When it was time for the Pueblo people to plant crops, everyone helped. The men kept the weeds pulled. Native Americans prayed for rain to make their crops grow. As part of their worship, they also had special dances called rain dances. When it was time for harvest, the women helped.

The land was bountiful to the Pueblo people. They grew many different crops. They planted beans, squash and 19 different kinds of corn. They gathered wild nuts and berries. They hunted for deer and rabbits. They also traded with other tribes for things they could not grow or hunt.

The Pueblo people lived in unusual houses. Their homes were made of adobe brick. Adobe is a type of mud. They shaped the mud into bricks, dried them, then built with them. Many adobe homes exist today in the Southwest.

The adobe homes of long ago had no doors. The Pueblo people entered through a type of trapdoor at the top. The homes were three or four stories high. The ground floor had no windows and was used for storage. These adobe homes were clustered around a central plaza. Each village had several clusters of homes. Villages also had two or three clubhouses where people could gather for celebrations. Each village also had places for worship.

1. What were the five states where the Pueblo people lived? Colorado, California, Arizona, New Mexico, and Utah.

2. What were three crops the Pueblo people grew? Beans, 19 types of corn, and squash.

3. The early pueblo houses had no

☐ yards.   ☐ windows.   ☑ doors.

Name: _____

Recognizing Details: The Pueblo People

"At the edge of the world
It grows light.
The trees stand shining."
(Pueblo poem)

Directions: Read more about the Pueblo people. Then answer the questions.

The Pueblo people were peaceful. They loved nature, and they seldom fought in wars. When they did fight, it was to protect their people or their land. Their dances, too, were gentle. The Pueblo people danced to ask the gods to bring rain or sunshine. Sometimes they asked the gods to help the women have children.

Some Native Americans wore masks when they danced. The masks were called kachinas (ka-chee-nas). They represented the faces of dead ancestors. (Ancestors are all the family members who have lived and died before.)

The Pueblo people were talented at crafts. The men of many tribes made beautiful jewelry. The women made pottery and painted it with beautiful colors. They traded some of the things they made with people from other tribes.

Both boys and girls needed their parents' permission to marry. After they married, they were given a room next to the bride's mother. If the marriage did not work out, sometimes the groom moved back home again.

1. Among the Pueblo people, who made jewelry? _____

2. Who made pottery? _____

3. What did some of the Pueblo people wear when they danced? _____

_____

4. Why did the Pueblo people dance for the gods? _____

_____

5. Where did newly married couples live? _____

_____

6. Why would a man move back home after marriage? _____

_____

Recognizing Details: The Pueblo People

Directions: Review what you learned about the Pueblo people. Then answer the questions.

1. How many different tribes lived in the Southwestern part of the United States? _____

2. The article specifically names three of the Pueblo tribes. Where could you find the names of the other Pueblo tribes?

_____

_____

3. How did the Pueblo people build their adobe homes? _____

_____

4. How did the location and climate affect their lifestyle? _____

_____

_____

_____

5. How were the jobs of the men and women of a Pueblo tribe alike? _____

_____

_____

6. How were their jobs different? _____

_____

7. How do the responsibilities of the Pueblo men and women discussed differ from those of men and women today?

_____

_____

_____

_____

Comprehension: A California Tribe

Directions: Read about the Yuma. Then answer the questions.

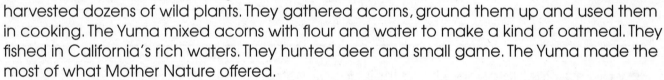

California was home to many Native Americans. The weather was warm, and food was plentiful. California was an ideal place to live.

One California tribe that made good use of the land was the Yuma. The Yuma farmed and gathered roots and berries. They harvested dozens of wild plants. They gathered acorns, ground them up and used them in cooking. The Yuma mixed acorns with flour and water to make a kind of oatmeal. They fished in California's rich waters. They hunted deer and small game. The Yuma made the most of what Mother Nature offered.

The Yuma lived in huts. The roofs were made of dirt. The walls were made of grass. Some Yuma lived together in big round buildings made with poles and woven grasses. As many as 50 people lived in these large homes.

Like other tribes, the Yuma made crafts. Their woven baskets were especially beautiful. The women also wove cradles, hats, bowls and other useful items for the tribe.

When it was time to marry, a boy's parents chose a 15-year-old girl for him. The girl was a Yuma, too, but from another village. Except for the chief, each man took only one wife.

When a Yuma died, a big ceremony was held. The Yumas had great respect for death. After someone died, his or her name was never spoken again.

1. What were two reasons why California was an ideal place to live?

_____

_____

2. What did the Yuma use acorns for? _____

_____

3. What was a beautiful craft made by the Yuma? _____

4. How old was a Yuma bride? _____

5. What types of homes did the Yuma live in? _____

6. How did the Yuma feel about death? _____

_____

Name: _____

Recognizing Details: The Yuma

Directions: Review what you read about the Yuma. Write the answers.

1. How did the Yuma make good use of the land?

_____

_____

2. How were the Yuma like the Pueblo people? _____

_____

_____

3. How were they different? _____

_____

_____

4. Why did the Yuma have homes different than those of the Pueblo tribes?

_____

_____

5. When it was time for a young Yuma man to marry, his parents selected a fifteen-year-old bride for him from another tribe. Do you think this is a good idea? Why or why not?

_____

_____

6. Why do you suppose the Yuma never spoke a person's name after he/she died?

_____

_____

7. Do you think this would be an easy thing to do? Explain your answer. _____

_____

Name: _____

Following Directions: Sailor Native Americans

Directions: Read about the Sailor Native Americans of Puget Sound. Then work the puzzle.

Three tribes lived on Puget (pew-jit) Sound in Washington state. They made their living from the sea. People later called them the "Sailor" Indians.

These Native Americans fished for salmon. They trapped the salmon in large baskets. Sometimes they used large nets. The sea was filled with fish. Their nets rarely came up empty.

The Sailor Native Americans also gathered roots and berries. They hunted deer, black bear and ducks.

Their homes were amazing! They built big wooden buildings without nails. They did not use saws to cut the wood. The walls and roofs were tied together. Each building had different homes inside. As many as 50 families lived in each big building.

Across:

1. The three tribes on Puget Sound were called the "_____" Native Americans.

2. The _____ and roofs of their buildings were tied together.

4. Because their buildings were tied together, they did not need _____.

Down:

1. Type of fish the "Sailor" Native Americans caught

3. As many as _____ families could live in their big buildings.

5. The buildings were put together without using _____ to cut the wood.

Following Directions: Sailor Native Americans

Directions: Review what you read about the Sailor Native Americans. Write your answers.

1. How were the housing arrangements of the Puget Sound Native Americans similar to those of the Yuma?

   _____

2. How was the diet of the Sailor Native Americans like those of the Yuma and Pueblo?

   _____

3. How was it different? _____

   _____

4. The Sailor Native Americans made a living from the sea, and their nets were rarely empty. What type of transportation do you think these Native Americans used to get their nets to the sea?

   _____

5. Where could you find more information on this group of Native Americans to check your answer?

   _____

6. Verify your answer. Were you correct? _____

7. Who do you think performed the many tasks in the Sailor village? Write men, women, boys and/or girls for your answers.

   Built homes? _____   Made fishing baskets? _____

   Fished? _____   Gathered roots and berries? _____

   Hunted game? _____   Made fishing nets? _____

7. The homes of the Sailor Native Americans could be compared to what type of modern dwelling?

   _____

Recognizing Details: The Woodlands People

Directions: Read about the Woodlands People. Then answer the questions.

The Southeast Woodlands people lived in a huge wooded area. The 15 tribes that lived in the Southeast Woodlands were very different from the Pueblo people of the Southwest.

The Woodlands people liked war. Boys could not wait to grow up and become warriors! It was a mark of manhood to fight. They carried clubs and shields. They used bows, arrows and long spears. Many of the Woodlands people took the scalps of their victims.

Many warriors had tattoos. Tattoos are pictures on the skin. Tattoos were marks of bravery in battle. A man with many tattoos was a hero.

These Southeast Woodlands people lived in different types of homes. Because it was hot, the houses of some tribes in what is now Florida did not have walls. The Seminole (sem-in-ole) houses had floors raised off the ground. The roofs were made of reeds, which are a type of grass.

In warm weather, the Woodlands people often went barefoot. In cold weather, they wore moccasins (mock-ah-sins) on their feet. Men wore buckskin pants and women wore buckskin skirts. Their clothes were made from the hides of deer. When it was very cold, they wore beaver robes to keep warm.

1. What are two ways the Woodlands people were different from the Pueblos?

_____

_____

2. What are four things the Woodlands people used in battle?

_____

_____

Directions: Check the correct answer.

3. In warm weather, Woodland Native Americans

☐ wore moccasins.　　☐ went barefoot.　　☐ wore cowboy boots.

4. When it was cold, they wrapped themselves in

☐ beaver robes.　　☐ cotton shawls.　　☐ buffalo robes.

Name: _____

Sequencing: Kanati's Son

A **legend** is a story or group of stories handed down through generations. Legends are usually about an actual person.

Directions: Read about Kanati's son. Then number the events in order.

This legend is told by a tribe called the Cherokee (chair-oh-key).

Long ago, soon after the world was made, a hunter and his wife lived on a big mountain with their son. The father's name was Kanati (kah-na-tee), which means "lucky hunter." The mother's name was Selu (see-loo), which means "corn." No one remembers the son's name.

The little boy used to play alone by the river each day. One day, elders of the tribe told the boy's parents they had heard two children playing. Since their boy was the only child around, the parents were puzzled. They told their son what the elders had said.

"I do have a playmate," the boy said. "He comes out of the water. He says he is the brother that mother threw in the river."

Then Selu knew what had happened.

"He is formed from the blood of the animals I washed in the river," she told Kanati. "After you kill them, I wash them in the river before I cook them."

Here is what Kanati told his boy: "Tomorrow when the other boy comes, wrestle with him. Hold him to the ground and call for us."

The boy did as his parents told him. When he called, they came running and grabbed the wild boy. They took him home and tried to tame him. The boy grew up with magic powers. The Cherokee called this "adawehi" (ad-da-we-hi). He was always getting into mischief! But he saved himself with his magic.

_____ Selu and Kanati try to tame the boy from the river.

_____ The little boy tells Selu and Kanati about the other boy.

_____ The little boy's parents are puzzled.

_____ The new boy grows up with magic powers.

_____ The elders tell Selu and Kanati they heard two children playing.

_____ The little boy wrestles his new playmate to the ground.

Comprehension: "Why Owls Have Big Eyes"

Directions: Read the Native American legend "Why Owls Have Big Eyes." Then answer the questions.

Creator made all the animals, one by one. He made each one the way they wanted to look. Owl interrupted when Creator was making Rabbit.

"Whooo, whooo," he said. "Make me now. I want a long neck like Swan, red feathers like Cardinal and a sharp beak like Eagle. Make me the most beautiful bird in the world."

"Quiet!" shouted Creator. "I am making Rabbit. Turn around and wait your turn."

Creator made Rabbit's long ears and long back legs. Before he could make Rabbit's long front legs, Owl interrupted again.

"Whooo, whooo," Owl said. "Make me now. Make me the most beautiful bird in the world."

"Close your eyes. No one may watch me work," said Creator. "Wait your turn. Do not interrupt again."

Owl would not wait. He was very rude. "I will watch if I want to," he said.

"All right then," said Creator. "I will make you now."

He pushed Owl's head until it was close to his body. He shook Owl until his eyes grew big with fright. He pulled on Owl's ears so they stuck out on both sides. Then he covered Owl's feathers with mud.

"There," he said. "That's what you get for not waiting your turn. You have big ears to listen so you can hear when you are told what to do. You have big eyes, but you can't watch me with them. I work only in the day and you will be awake only at night. Your feathers will forever be the color of mud, not red like Cardinal's."

When he heard Creator's words, Owl flew away. Creator turned to finish Rabbit, but Rabbit had run away before Creator could finish his front legs or give him sharp claws to defend himself. To this day, rabbits have short front legs, are afraid of owls and cannot defend themselves. And that's why owls have short necks, big eyes, brownish feathers and ears that stick out.

1. According to this legend, who made all the animals?_____

2. Why did Rabbit run away before Creator finished making him?

_____

_____

3. Why didn't Creator make Owl beautiful? _____

_____

4. Why are rabbits afraid of owls? _____

Review

Review what you read about Native Americans. Then answer the questions.

1. Of the tribes discussed, which one would you most like to have been a member of? Explain your answer.

_____

_____

2. Why did each of the tribes have a different lifestyle? _____

_____

_____

3. How did their location influence how each of the tribes functioned? _____

_____

_____

Directions: Select two of the Native American tribes you read about. Compare and contrast their homes, clothing and lifestyle in the Venn diagram. Write words and phrases that were unique to one group or the other in the correct parts of the circle. Write words and phrases that are common to both groups in the section where the circles intersect.

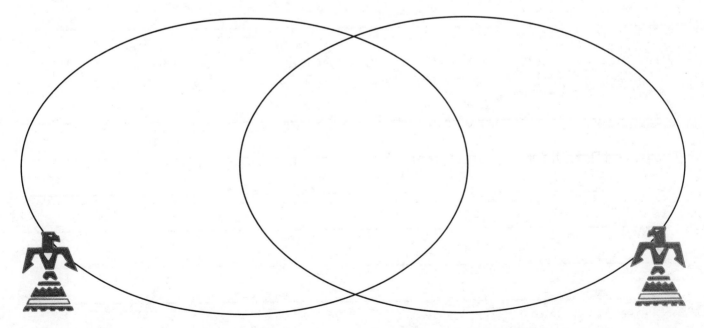

Review

Directions: Review what you learned about Native Americans. Write your answers on the lines.

1. Select one of the Native American tribes and write about how their lives would be different today.

_____

_____

_____

_____

2. Do research using an encyclopedia, books on Native Americans or on the Internet. Find out how some of these tribes are living today. Write a short paragraph about what you learned.

_____

_____

_____

_____

_____

3. Use reference sources to learn about Native Americans that once lived in your area. Write a paragraph describing their lifestyle.

_____

_____

_____

_____

_____

Main Idea: "The Hare and the Tortoise"

The story of "The Hare and the Tortoise" is called a **fable.** Fables are usually short stories. As you read this story and the other fables on the next few pages, look for two characteristics the fables have in common.

Directions: Read the fable "The Hare and the Tortoise." Then answer the questions.

One day the hare and the tortoise were talking. Or rather, the hare was bragging and the tortoise was listening.

"I am faster than the wind," bragged the hare. "I feel sorry for you because you are so slow! Why, you are the slowest fellow I have ever seen."

"Do you think so?" asked the tortoise with a smile. "I will race you to that big tree across the field."

Slowly, he lifted a leg. Slowly, he pointed toward the tree.

"Ha!" scoffed the hare. "You must be kidding! You will most certainly be the loser! But, if you insist, we will race."

The tortoise nodded politely. "I'll be off," he said. Slowly and steadily, the tortoise moved across the field.

The hare stood back and laughed. "How sad that he should compete with me!" he said. His chest puffed up with pride. "I will take a little nap while the poor old tortoise lumbers along. When I wake up, he will still be only halfway across the field."

The tortoise kept on, slow and steady, across the field. Some time later, the hare awoke. He discovered that while he slept, the tortoise had won the race.

1. What is the main idea? (Check one.)

_____ Tortoises are faster than hares.

_____ Hares need more sleep than tortoises.

_____ Slow and steady wins the race.

2. The hare brags that he is faster than what? (Check one.)

_____ a bullet

_____ a greyhound

_____ the wind

3. Who is modest, the tortoise or the hare? _____

Cause and Effect: "The Hare and the Tortoise"

Another important skill in reading is recognizing cause and effect. The **cause** is the reason something happens. The **effect** is what happens or the situation that results from the cause. In the story, the hare falling asleep is a cause. It causes the hare to lose the race. Losing the race is the effect.

Directions: Identify the underlined words or phrases by writing **cause** or **effect** on the blanks.

1. <u>The hare and tortoise had a race</u> because the hare bragged about being faster.

   _____

2. The tortoise won the race <u>because he continued on, slowly, but steadily.</u>

   _____

Directions: Review the fable "The Hare and the Tortoise." Then answer the questions.

1. Who are the two main characters? _____

2. Where does the story take place? _____

3. What lessons can be learned from this story? _____

   _____

4. The lesson that is learned at the end of a fable has a special name. What is that special name?

   _____

5. Why did the hare want to race the tortoise? _____

   _____

6. How do you think the hare felt at the end of the story? _____

   _____

7. How do you think the tortoise felt at the end of the story? _____

   _____

   _____

   _____

24

Name: _____

Sequencing: "The Fox and the Crow"

Directions: Read the fable "The Fox and the Crow." Then number the events in order.

Once upon a time, a crow found a piece of cheese on the ground. "Aha!" he said to himself. "This dropped from a workman's sandwich. It will make a fine lunch for me."

The crow picked up the cheese in his beak. He flew to a tree to eat it. Just as he began to chew it, a fox trotted by.

"Hello, crow!" he said slyly, for he wanted the cheese. The fox knew if the crow answered, the cheese would fall from its mouth. Then the fox would have cheese for lunch!

The crow just nodded.

"It's a wonderful day, isn't it?" asked the fox.

The crow nodded again and held onto the cheese.

"You are the most beautiful bird I have ever seen," added the fox.

The crow spread his feathers. Everyone likes a compliment. Still, the crow held firmly to the cheese.

"There is something I have heard," said the fox, "and I wonder if it is true. I heard that you sing more sweetly than any of the other birds."

The crow was eager to show off his talents. He opened his beak to sing. The cheese dropped to the ground.

"I said you were beautiful," said the fox as he ran away with the cheese. "I did not say you were smart!"

_____ The crow drops the cheese.

_____ The crow flies to a tree with the cheese.

_____ The fox tells the crow he is beautiful.

_____ The fox runs off with the cheese.

_____ A workman loses the cheese from his sandwich.

_____ The fox comes along.

_____ The fox tells the crow he has heard that crows sing beautifully.

_____ The crow picks up the cheese.

Name: _____

Predicting: "The Fox and the Crow"

Directions: Review the fable "The Fox and the Crow." Then answer the questions.

1. With what words does the story begin? _____

2. What other type of story often begins with these same words? _____

3. Although it is not stated, where do you think the story takes place?

_____

4. How does the fox get what he wants from the crow? _____

_____

_____

5. How is the crow in this story like the hare in the last fable? _____

_____

_____

Predicting is telling or guessing what you think might happen in a story or situation based on what you already know.

Directions: Write predictions to answer these questions.

6. Based on what you read, what do you think the crow will do the next time he finds a piece of cheese?

_____

_____

7. What do you think the fox will do the next time he wants to trick the crow? _____

_____

_____

_____

_____

Name: _____

Following Directions: "The Boy Who Cried Wolf"

Directions: Read the fable "The Boy Who Cried Wolf." Then complete the puzzle.

Once there was a shepherd boy who tended his sheep alone. Sheep are gentle animals. They are easy to take care of. The boy grew bored.

"I can't stand another minute alone with these sheep," he said crossly. He knew only one thing would bring people quickly to him. If he cried, "Wolf!" the men in the village would run up the mountain. They would come to help save the sheep from the wolf.

"Wolf!" he yelled loudly, and he blew on his horn.

Quick as a wink, a dozen men came running. When they realized it was a joke, they were very angry. The boy promised never to do it again. But a week later, he grew bored and cried, "Wolf!" again. Again, the men ran to him. This time they were very, very angry.

Soon afterwards, a wolf really came. The boy was scared. "Wolf!" he cried. "Wolf! Wolf! Wolf!"

He blew his horn, but no one came, and the wolf ate all his sheep.

Across:

2. This is where the boy tends sheep.

4. When no one came, the wolf _____ all the sheep.

5. Sheep are _____ and easy to take care of.

Down:

1. The people who come are from here.

2. At first, when the boy cries, "Wolf!" the _____ come running.

3. When a wolf really comes, this is how the boy feels.

Cause and Effect: "The Boy Who Cried Wolf"

Directions: Identify the underlined words as a cause or an effect.

1. <u>The boy cries wolf</u> because he is bored. _____

2. <u>The boy blows his horn</u> and the men come running. _____

3. No one comes, and <u>the wolf eats all the sheep</u>. _____

Directions: Answer the questions.

4. What lesson can be learned from this story? _____

_____

_____

_____

5. How is this story like the two other fables you read? _____

_____

_____

_____

6. Is the boy in the story more like the fox or the hare? How so? _____

_____

_____

_____

_____

_____

_____

Name: _____

Comprehension:
"The City Mouse and the Country Mouse"

Directions: Read the fable "The City Mouse and the Country Mouse." Then answer the questions.

Once there were two mice, a city mouse and a country mouse. They were cousins. The country mouse was always begging his cousin to visit him. Finally, the city mouse agreed.

When he arrived, the city mouse was not very polite. "How do you stand it here?" he asked, wrinkling his nose. "All you have to eat is corn and barley. All you have to wear is old, tattered work clothes. And all you have to listen to are the other animals. Why don't you come and visit me? Then you will see what it's like to really live!"

The country mouse liked corn and barley. He liked the sounds of the other animals. And he liked his old work clothes fine. Secretly, he thought his cousin was silly to wear fancy clothes. Still, the city sounded exciting. Why not give it a try?

Since he had no clothes to pack, the country mouse was ready in no time. His cousin told him stories about the city as they traveled. The buildings were so high! The food was so good! The girl mice were so beautiful!

The home of the city mouse was nice. He lived in a hole in the wall in an old castle. "It is only a hole in the wall," said the city mouse, "but it is a very nice wall, indeed!"

That night, the mice crept out of the wall. Everyone had eaten, but the maid had not cleaned up. The table was still loaded with good food. The mice ate and ate. The country mouse was not used to rich food. He began to feel sick to his stomach.

Just then, they heard loud barking. Two huge dogs ran into the room. They nearly bit off the country mouse's tail! He barely made it to the hole in the wall in time. That did it!

 "Thank you for showing me the city," said the country mouse, "but it is too exciting for me. I am going home where it is peaceful. I can't wait to settle my stomach with some corn and barley."

1. What are three things the city mouse says are wrong with the country? _____

_____

2. Why doesn't it take the country mouse long to get ready to leave with the city mouse?

_____

3. Why does the country mouse secretly think his cousin is silly? _____

Name: _____

Sequencing:
"The City Mouse and the Country Mouse"

Directions: Review the fable "The City Mouse and the Country Mouse." Use the Venn diagram to compare and contrast the lifestyles of the city mouse and the country mouse.

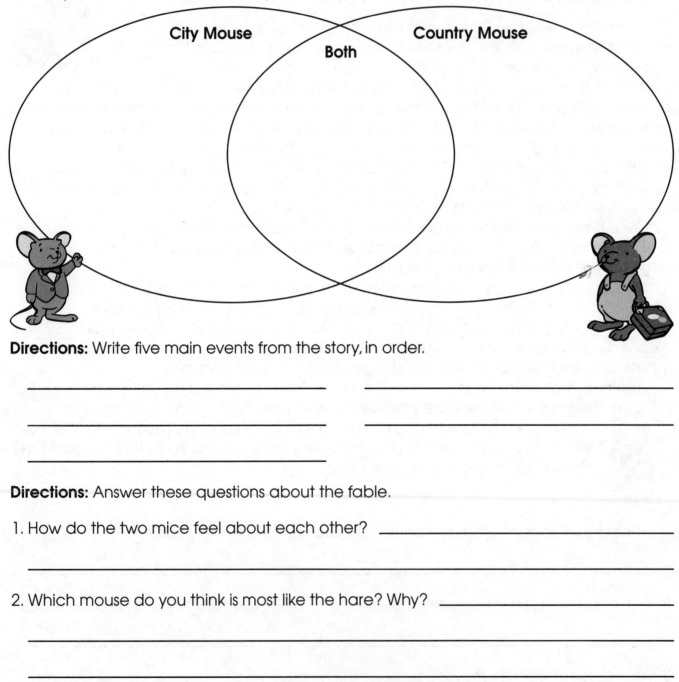

City Mouse   Both   Country Mouse

Directions: Write five main events from the story, in order.

_____   _____

_____   _____

_____

Directions: Answer these questions about the fable.

1. How do the two mice feel about each other? _____

_____

2. Which mouse do you think is most like the hare? Why? _____

_____

_____

Sequencing: "The Man and the Snake"

Directions: Read the fable "The Man and the Snake." Then number the events in order.

Once, a kind man saw a snake in the road. It was winter and the poor snake was nearly frozen. The man began to walk away, but he could not.

"The snake is one of Earth's creatures, too," he said. He picked up the snake and put it in a sack. "I will take it home to warm up by my fire. Then I will set it free."

The man stopped for lunch at a village inn. He put his coat and his sack on a bench by the fireplace. He planned to sit nearby, but the inn was crowded, so he had to sit across the room.

He soon forgot about the snake. As he was eating his soup, he heard screams. Warmed by the fire, the snake had crawled from the bag. It hissed at the people near the fire.

The man jumped up and ran to the fireplace. "Is this how you repay the kindness of others?" he shouted.

He grabbed a stick used for stirring the fire and chased the snake out of the inn.

_____ The man puts his bag down by the fireplace.

_____ The man chases the snake.

_____ A kind man rescues the snake.

_____ The snake warms up and crawls out of the bag.

_____ The man plans to take the snake home.

_____ The man eats a bowl of soup.

_____ The snake hisses at people.

_____ A snake is nearly frozen in the road.

_____ The man grabs a stick from the fireplace.

Sequencing: "The Wind and the Sun"

Directions: Read the fable "The Wind and the Sun." Then number the events in order.

One day, North Wind and Sun began to argue about who was stronger.

"I am stronger," declared North Wind.

"No," said Sun. "I am much stronger than you."

They argued for three days and three nights.

Finally, Sun said, "I know how we can settle the argument. See that traveler walking down the road? Whoever can make him take off his cloak first is the stronger. Do you agree?"

North Wind agreed. He wanted to try first. He blew and blew. The traveler shivered and pulled his cloak tightly around his body. North Wind sent a blast of wind so strong it almost pulled the cloak off the traveler, but the traveler only held tighter to his cloak.

Then it was Sun's turn. When Sun sent gentle, warm sunbeams, the traveler loosened his cloak. Then Sun sent his warmest beams to the traveler. After a short time, the traveler became so warm he threw off his cloak and ran to the shade of the nearest tree.

_____ Sun sent warm beams to the traveler.

_____ Sun and North Wind argued.

_____ The traveler threw off his cloak and ran to the shade.

_____ The traveler pulled his cloak tightly around his body.

_____ North Wind blew cold air on the traveler.

Directions: Answer the questions. (Check one.)

What is the moral of this fable?

_____ Sun is stronger than North Wind.

_____ North Wind is cold.

_____ A kind and gentle manner works better than force.

_____ Travelers should hold on to their cloaks when the wind blows.

_____ Stay out of arguments between Sun and North Wind.

Who do you think is stronger, North Wind or Sun? Why? _____

_____

Name: _____

Review

At the beginning of the section on fables, you were asked to discover two elements common to the fables.

Directions: Review the fables you read. Then answer the questions.

1. What are the two elements common to fables?_____

_____

_____

2. Each fable has a "moral" or lesson to be learned. What is the moral of each of the fables?

"The Hare and the Tortoise" _____

"The Fox and the Crow" _____

"The Boy Who Cried Wolf" _____

"The City Mouse and the Country Mouse" _____

"The Man and the Snake"_____

3. How do the titles of the fables give clues to what or who the fables were about?

_____

_____

4. For each fable, write the character you think is the good character and the one you think is the bad character.

	"Good character"	"Bad character"
"The Hare and the Tortoise"	_____	_____
"The Fox and the Crow"	_____	_____
"The Wind and the Sun"	_____	_____
"The City Mouse and the Country Mouse"	_____	_____
"The Man and the Snake"	_____	_____

Fable Writing Organizer

Fables are short stories with animals as the main characters. Each story teaches a lesson.

Directions: Select one of the following pairs of animals as characters to use for a fable of your own.

A pig and an ox	An ant and a frog	A cat and a monkey
A fly and a butterfly	A spider and a bear	A goose and a deer
A snail and a lion	A horse and a dog	A T-Rex and a shark

Directions: Fill in the outline below with words and phrases to organize a fable of your own.

Animal pair _____

Type of conflict between the animals _____

_____

_____

How the conflict is settled _____

_____

_____

_____

Moral of the story _____

_____

Directions: Write your fable. Give your fable a title. Illustrate it if you like.

_____

_____

_____

_____

_____

_____

_____

Recognizing Details:
"Why Bear Has a Short Tail"

Some stories try to explain the reasons why certain things occur in nature.

Directions: Read the legend "Why Bear Has a Short Tail." Then answer the questions.

Long ago, Bear had a long tail like Fox. One winter day, Bear met Fox coming out of the woods. Fox was carrying a long string of fish. He had stolen the fish, but that is not what he told Bear.

"Where did you get those fish?" asked Bear, rubbing his paws together. Bear loved fish. It was his favorite food.

"I was out fishing and caught them," replied Fox.

Bear did not know how to fish. He had only tasted fish that others gave him. He was eager to learn to catch his own.

"Please Fox, will you tell me how to fish?" asked Bear.

So, the mean old Fox said to Bear, "Cut a hole in the ice and stick your tail in the hole. It will get cold, but soon the fish will begin to bite. When you can stand it no longer, pull your tail out. It will be covered with fish!"

"Will it hurt?" asked Bear, patting his tail.

"It will hurt some," admitted Fox. "But the longer you leave your tail in the water, the more fish you will catch."

Bear did as Fox told him. He loved fish, so he left his tail in the icy water a very, very long time. The ice froze around Bear's tail. When he pulled free, his tail remained stuck in the ice. That is why bears today have short tails.

1. How does Fox get his string of fish? _____

2. What does he tell Bear to do? _____

_____

3. Why does Bear do as Fox told him? _____

_____

4. How many fish does Bear catch? _____

5. What happens when Bear tries to pull his tail out? _____

_____

Recognizing Details:
"Why Bear Has a Short Tail"

Directions: Review the legend "Why Bear Has a Short Tail." Then answer the questions.

1. When Bear asks Fox where he got his fish, is Fox truthful in his response? Why or why not?

_____

_____

2. Why does Bear want to know how to fish? _____

_____

3. In reality, are bears able to catch their own fish? How? _____

_____

4. Is Bear very smart to believe Fox? Why or why not? _____

_____

5. How would you have told Bear to catch his own fish? _____

_____

6. What is one word you would use to describe Fox? _____

   Explain your answer. _____

_____

7. What is one word you would use to describe Bear? _____

   Explain your answer. _____

_____

8. Is this story realistic? _____

9. Could it have really happened? Explain your answer. _____

_____

Predicting: "How the Donkey Got Long Ears"

Directions: Write your predictions to answer these questions.

1. How do you think animals got their names? _____

_____

2. Why would it be confusing if animals did not have names? _____

_____

Directions: Read the legend "How the Donkey Got Long Ears." Then answer the questions.

    In the beginning when the world was young, animals had no names. It was very confusing! A woman would say, "Tell the thingamajig to bring in the paper." The man would say, "What thingamajig?" She was talking about the dog, of course, but the man didn't know that.

    Together, they decided to name the animals on their farm. First, they named their pet thingamajig Dog. They named the pink thingamajig that oinked Pig. They named the red thingamajig that crowed Rooster. They named the white thingamajig that laid eggs Hen. They named the little yellow thingamajigs that cheeped Chicks. They named the big brown thingamajig they rode Horse.

    Then they came to another thingamajig. It looked like Horse, but was smaller. It would be confusing to call the smaller thingamajig Horse, they decided.

    "Let's name it Donkey," said the woman. So they did.

    Soon all the animals knew their names. All but Donkey, that is. Donkey kept forgetting.

    "What kind of a thingamajig am I again?" he would ask the man.

    "You are Donkey!" the man would answer. Each time Donkey forgot, the man tugged on Donkey's ears to help him remember.

    Soon, however, Donkey would forget his name again.

    "Uh, what's my name?" he would ask the woman.

    She would answer, "Donkey! Donkey! Donkey!" and pull his ears each time. She was a clever woman but not very patient.

    At first, the man and woman did not notice that Donkey's ears grew longer each time they were pulled. Donkey was patient but not very clever. It took him a long time to learn his name. By the time he remembered his name was Donkey, his ears were much longer than Horse's ears. That is why donkeys have long ears.

3. What words could you use to describe Donkey? _____

    Explain your choice. _____

Comprehension:
"How the Donkey Got Long Ears"

Directions: Review the legend "How the Donkey Got Long Ears." Then answer the questions.

1. What do the man and woman call the animals before they have names?

   _____

2. Why do they decide to name the animals? _____

   _____

3. What is the first animal they name? _____

4. Besides being impatient, what else is the woman? _____

5. What did the people do each time they reminded Donkey of his name? _____

   _____

6. Which thingamajigs are yellow? _____

7. Which thingamajig is pink? _____

8. What is the thingamajig they ride? _____

9. Why don't they call the donkey Horse? _____

Directions: Imagine that you are the one who gets to name the animals. Write names for these new "animals."

10. A thingamajig with yellow spots that swims _____

11. A thingamajig with large ears, a short tail and six legs _____

12. A thingamajig with purple wings that flies and sings sweet melodies

    _____

13. A thingamajig that gives chocolate milk _____

    _____

Following Directions: Puzzling Out the Animals

Directions: Review the legend "How the Donkey Got Long Ears." Then work the puzzle.

Name: _____

Across:

3. Is the woman patient?
4. This thingamajig cheeps.
5. This thingamajig lays eggs.
6. Is the woman clever?
7. This thingamajig is pink.

Down:

1. This animal can't remember its name.
2. This is what the animals are called before they have names.
5. People ride this brown animal.

Review

Rudyard Kipling wrote many legends explaining such things as why bears have short tails, how the camel got his hump and why a leopard has spots. He wrote his stories in a book called *Just So Stories for Little Children*. You can find a copy of Kipling's book at the library or a bookstore.

Directions: Think about how animals look and behave. Using your wildest imagination, write a short explanation for the following situations.

1. Why the pig has a short tail _____

_____

2. How the elephant got his big ears _____

_____

3. Why birds fly _____

_____

4. Why rabbits are timid _____

_____

5. How the giraffe got a long neck _____

_____

6. How the mouse got his tail _____

_____

Directions: Illustrate one of your stories as a three- or four-panel cartoon.

Comprehension: "Why Cats and Dogs Fight"

Directions: Read the legend "Why Cats and Dogs Fight." Then answer the questions.

Long ago, Cat and Dog were friends. They played together. They ate together. They even slept near one another.

Yes, Cat and Dog got along very well! The reason was simple. All the other animals had to work for humans. But because Cat was so clean, it did not have to work. And because Dog was so loyal, it did not have to work either. Cat and Dog were the only animals who had time to play. They enjoyed themselves very much.

Everything was too good to be true! Cat and Dog wanted to make sure their lives stayed easy. They asked the old man and woman who owned them to sign a paper saying they would never have to work. That way, they would have proof that they could spend their lives at play.

The old man and woman signed the paper. Then Dog buried it in the ground with his bones. After their masters died, the other animals grew more and more jealous.

"The people aren't here any more to protect them. Why should they get off so easy?" Ox asked Cow.

"You're right," said Cow. "Let's find that paper and destroy it. Then there will be no proof that Cat and Dog can play. They will have to work like we do."

Ox and Cow looked everywhere, but they could not find the paper. Finally, they asked Rat to help. Rat sniffed and sniffed. At last, he smelled the paper. He pulled it from the ground and gave it to Ox. Ox ground it under his hoof and destroyed it. Then Dog had to go to work as a hunter. Cat had to catch mice. Cat never forgave Dog for burying the paper in a spot Rat could find. To this day, that's why cats and dogs fight.

1. Why didn't Cat have to work? _____

2. Why didn't Dog have to work? _____

3. What animals talk about finding the paper? _____

4. Who destroys the paper? _____

5. Who finds the paper? _____

Name: _____

Comprehension: "Why Cats and Dogs Fight"

Directions: Review the legend "Why Cats and Dogs Fight." Then answer the questions.

1. What do Cat and Dog do to make sure their life stays easy? _____

_____

_____

2. Does their plan work? _____

3. Why not? _____

4. When does the easy time stop for the cat and dog? _____

5. Cat gets mad at Dog for burying the paper in a place where Rat can easily find it. Do you think Dog also gets mad at Cat? Explain your answer.

_____

_____

6. What other animal pair could you compare to Cat and Dog? _____

7. Why did you select this animal pair? _____

8. Does the quarreling of Dog and Cat with the other animals remind you of your own quarrels with your brothers or sisters? Explain.

_____

_____

_____

9. What if Rat never found the paper? Rewrite the end of the story, beginning with these words: "And to this day, that's why cats and dogs . . ."

_____

_____

_____

Main Idea: "The Sly Fox"

Directions: Read the legend "The Sly Fox." Then answer the questions.

One evening, Fox met Wolf in the forest. Wolf was in a terrible mood. He felt hungry, too. So he said to Fox, "Don't move! I'm going to eat you this minute."

As he spoke, Wolf backed Fox up against a tree. Fox realized she couldn't run away.

"I will have to use my wits instead of my legs," she thought to herself.

Aloud to Wolf, Fox said calmly, "I would have made a good dinner for you last year. But I've had three little babies since then. I spend all my time looking for food to feed them."

Before she could go on, Wolf interrupted. "I don't care how many children you have! I'm going to eat you right now." Wolf began closing in on Fox.

"Stop!" shouted Fox. "Look how skinny I am. I ran off all my fat looking for food for my children. But I know where you can find something that's good and fat!" Wolf backed off to listen.

"There's a well near here. In the bottom of it is a big fat piece of cheese. I don't like cheese, so it's of no use to me. Come, I'll show you."

Wolf trotted off after Fox, making sure she could not run away.

"See," said Fox when they got to the well.

Inside was what looked like a round yellow piece of cheese. It was really the moon's reflection, but Wolf didn't know this. Wolf leaned over the well, wondering how to get the cheese. Fox jumped up quickly and pushed Wolf in.

"I am a sly, old thing," Fox chuckled as she trotted home to her children. And to this day, that's why foxes are sly.

1. What is the main idea of this legend? (Check one.)

_____ Fox is cornered but uses her wits to outsmart Wolf and save her own life.

_____ Wolf is in a terrible mood and wants to eat Fox.

_____ Wolf thinks the moon was made of cheese.

2. Why did Fox say she will not make a good meal for Wolf? _____

_____

_____

3. What happens to Wolf at the end? _____

_____

Name: _____

Recognizing Details: "The Sly Fox"

Directions: Review the legend "The Sly Fox." Then answer the questions.

1. What are three events in the story that show Wolf's bad mood? _____

_____

_____

_____

2. What does Fox say she will have to use to get away from Wolf? _____

3. Where does Fox tell Wolf he can find a nice fat meal? _____

_____

4. How does Fox finally rid herself of Wolf? _____

5. What does Fox say as she trots home? _____

6. Have you ever been in a situation where you used words to solve a problem instead of fighting with someone? Write about it.

_____

_____

_____

7. In addition to teaching why foxes are sly, what other lesson does this story teach?

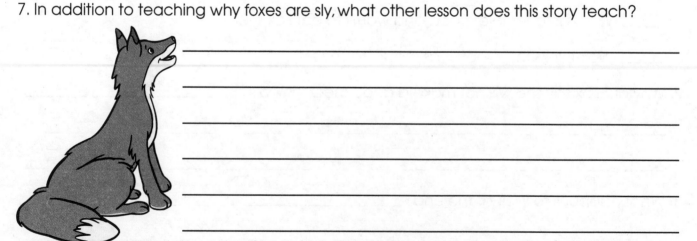

_____

_____

_____

_____

_____

Name: _____

Comprehension: "King of the Beasts"

Directions: Read the legend "King of the Beasts." Then answer the questions.

Once, a shy little rabbit was sleeping under a palm tree. Suddenly, a coconut fell and startled the rabbit awake. The rabbit began to twitch and worry.

"What was that awful noise?" he said. He looked around but didn't see the coconut. "The Earth must be breaking apart. Oh dear, oh dear, oh dear."

The little rabbit began running in circles. Soon a monkey joined him.

"Why are you running?" the monkey asked, trotting along beside the rabbit.

"The Earth is breaking apart, and I'm trying to escape," panted the little rabbit.

They were joined by a deer, a fox and an elephant. When they heard the Earth was breaking up, they all followed the rabbit. Soon a huge herd of animals was running in a circle.

"What's going on?" roared the lion to the elephant when he saw the herd.

"The Earth is breaking up!" shouted the elephant. "We are trying to escape."

The lion looked around. Except for all the dust, everything looked fine.

"Who said the Earth is breaking up?" he roared back to the elephant.

"The fox told me!" the elephant replied.

The lion asked the fox, and the fox said the deer told him. The deer said the monkey had told him. Finally, the lion traced the story to the rabbit.

"Show me the place!" the lion demanded.

The rabbit led the lion back to the palm tree. Right away, the lion saw the coconut on the ground.

"Silly rabbit!" he roared. "What you heard was a coconut falling. Go and tell the other animals they are safe."

The rabbit rushed to tell the other animals. They stopped running.

"The lion is smart!" said the monkey. "Let's name him 'King of the Beasts.'" So they did.

1. What kind of tree is the rabbit sleeping under? _____

2. Why does he think the Earth is breaking up? _____

_____

_____

3. Which animal is the first to join the rabbit? _____

4. What does the lion call the rabbit? _____

5. Who suggests naming the lion "King of the Beasts"? _____

Name: _____

Comprehension: "King of the Beasts"

Directions: Review the legend "King of the Beasts." Then answer the questions.

1. How does the lion become "King of the Beasts"? _____

_____

2. Instead of panicking about the Earth breaking apart, what should the rabbit have done?

_____

_____

_____

3. Instead of following the rabbit around in a circle, what should the monkey, deer and fox have done?

_____

_____

_____

4. Do you think naming the lion "King of the Beasts" was a good idea? Why or why not?

_____

_____

_____

5. What does this story teach you about peer pressure? Explain.

_____

_____

_____

_____

Name: _____

Recognizing Details: "Lazy Sheep"

Directions: Read the poem about the lazy sheep. Then answer the questions.

"Lazy sheep, please tell me why

In the grassy field you lie?

You eat and sleep away your day

While people work and sweat for pay!"

"Boy, do not talk to me so mean!"

Replied the sheep, so white he gleamed.

"I'm busy growing wool that's new

To spin into some clothes for you!"

The boy looked sad, his face got red.

"I'm sorry for the things I said!"

1. Why does the boy accuse the sheep of being lazy? _____

_____

2. What is the sheep actually doing? _____

_____

3. Where does the boy see the sheep? _____

_____

4. Why does the boy look sad? _____

_____

5. How does the boy apologize? _____

_____

Name: _____

Main Idea: "The Mouse"

Directions: Read the story "The Mouse." Then answer the questions.

One day when the cat and mouse were playing, the cat bit off the mouse's tail.

"Ouch!" cried the mouse. "Give me back my tail this instant!"

"I'll give your tail back when you go to the cow and bring me some milk!" replied the cat.

She held the mouse's tail high so the mouse could not reach it.

Right away, the mouse went to ask the cow for milk.

"I'll give you milk if you go to the farmer and get me some hay," said the cow.

When the mouse asked the farmer for hay, he said: "I'll give you hay if you go to the butcher and get me some meat."

The mouse wanted her tail back, so she went to the butcher. "I'll give you meat if you go to the baker and bring me some bread," said the butcher.

The mouse went to the baker, who said, "I'll give you bread. But if you get into my grain, I'll cut off your head!" The mouse quickly promised never to get into the baker's grain.

Then the baker gave the mouse bread. The mouse gave the bread to the butcher and the butcher gave the mouse meat. The mouse gave the meat to the farmer and the farmer gave the mouse hay. The mouse gave the hay to the cow and the cow gave the mouse milk. The mouse gave the cat milk and—finally!—the mouse got her tail back!

1. The main idea is: (Check one.)

——— To get what you want, you must be persistent.

——— A mouse's tail is worth a lot of work to a mouse.

——— Everybody is greedy, especially the baker.

2. What does the mouse promise the baker never to get into? _____

Directions: Fill in the blanks to show the steps the mouse follows to get her tail back.

3. She gets bread from the baker and gives it to _____ .

4. She gets meat from the butcher and gives it to _____ .

5. She gets hay from the farmer and gives it to _____ .

6. She gets milk from the cow and gives it to _____ .

7. That's when she _____ .

Sequencing: "The Mouse"

Directions: Review the story of "The Mouse." Then answer the questions.

1. Why do you think the cat does not simply give the tail back to the mouse when he asks for it?

_____

_____

_____

2. Have you ever done anything similar to a brother, sister or friend when they asked for something? Explain.

_____

_____

_____

_____

Directions: List the things the mouse has to do to get his tail back.

First _____

_____

Second _____

_____

Third _____

_____

Fourth _____

_____

Fifth _____

_____

Name: _____

Review

Directions: Review the fables and legends you read. Then write your answers.

1. Explain how "The Mouse" and "The Sly Fox" are similar stories. _____

_____

_____

_____

2. Explain how "King of the Beasts" and "The Sheep" are different stories. _____

_____

_____

_____

3. Compare and contrast the rabbit to the mouse. _____

_____

_____

_____

4. Compare and contrast one animal legend with one animal fable. _____

_____

_____

_____

5. Read one of Kipling's *Just So Stories*. Write your reaction to the story. _____

_____

_____

_____

Name: _____

Animal Legend Organizer

Directions: Follow the instructions to write a legend of your own.

1. Select one of the following titles for your legend. Circle the one you plan to use.

How the Tiger Got Stripes   How the Elephant Got a Tusk

How the Giraffe Got a Long Neck   How the Kangaroo Got Her Pouch

How the Gazelle Got Twisty Horns   Why the Pig Has a Short Tail

How the Elephant Got Big Ears   Why Birds Fly

Why Rabbits Are Timid   How the Giraffe Got a Long Neck

How the Mouse Got a Long Tail   Why Fish Swim

2. Briefly explain the type of conflict that will be in your legend. _____

_____

_____

3. Write words and phrases to show events you plan to include in your legend. _____

_____

_____

4. Summarize how you plan to settle the conflict or solve the problem. _____

_____

_____

Directions: Write your legend. Give it a title. Illustrate it if you like.

_____

_____

_____

_____

_____

_____

Recognizing Details: Giraffes

Directions: Read about giraffes. Then answer the questions.

Giraffes are tall, beautiful, graceful animals that live in Africa. When they are grown, male giraffes are about 18 feet tall. Adult females are about 14 feet tall.

Giraffes are not fat animals, but because they are so big, they weigh a lot. The average male weighs 2,800 pounds. Females weigh about 400 pounds less. Giraffes reach their full height when they are four years old. They continue to gain weight until they are about eight years old.

If you have ever seen giraffes, you know their necks and legs are very long. They are not awkward, though! Giraffes can move very quickly. They like to jump over fences and streams. They do this gracefully. They do not trip over their long legs.

If they are frightened, they can run 35 miles an hour. When giraffes gallop, all four feet are sometimes off the ground! Usually, young and old giraffes pace along at about 10 miles an hour.

Giraffes are strong. They can use their back legs as weapons. A lion can run faster than a giraffe, but a giraffe can kill a lion with one quick kick from its back legs.

Giraffes do not look scary. Their long eyelashes make them look gentle. They usually have a curious look on their faces. Many people think they are cute. Do you?

1. What is the weight of a full-grown male giraffe? _____

2. What is the weight of an adult female? _____

3. When does a giraffe run 35 miles an hour? _____

4. What do giraffes use as weapons? _____

5. For how long do giraffes continue to gain weight?

_____

6. When do giraffes reach their full height?

_____

7. Use a dictionary. What does **gallop** mean?

_____

_____

Comprehension: More About Giraffes

Directions: Read more about giraffes. Then answer the questions.

Most people don't notice, but giraffes have different patterns of spots. Certain species of giraffes have small spots. Other species have large spots. Some species have spots that are very regular. You can tell where one spot ends and another begins. Other species have spots that are kind of blotchy. This means the spots are not set off from each other as clearly. There are many other kinds of spot patterns. The pattern of a giraffe's spots is called "markings." No two giraffes have exactly the same markings.

There is one very rare type of giraffe. It is totally black! Have you ever seen one? This kind of giraffe is called a melanistic (mell-an-iss-tick) giraffe. The name comes from the word "melanin," which is the substance in cells that gives them color. Giraffes' spots help them blend in with their surroundings. A black giraffe would not blend in well with tree trunks and leaves. Maybe that is why they are so rare.

Being able to blend with surroundings helps animals survive. If a lion can't see a giraffe, he certainly can't eat it. This is called "protective coloration." The animal's color helps protect it.

Another protection giraffes have is their keen eyesight. Their large eyes are on the sides of their heads. Giraffes see anything that moves. They can see another animal a mile away! It is very hard to sneak up on a giraffe. Those who try usually get a quick kick with a powerful back leg.

1. What are markings? _____

2. How far away can a giraffe see another animal? _____

3. Where are a giraffe's eyes? _____

4. What is protective coloration? _____

5. What color is the very rare type of giraffe? _____

6. How do giraffes protect themselves? _____

7. How many kinds of spot patterns do giraffes have? ☐ two   ☐ four   ☐ many

8. Use a dictionary. What does **species** mean? _____

_____

_____

Following Directions: Puzzling Out Giraffes

Directions: Review what you read about giraffes. Read more about giraffes below. Then work the puzzle.

Have you noticed that giraffes have a curious look? That is because they are always paying attention. Their lives depend upon it! Giraffes cannot save themselves from a lion if they don't see it. Giraffes look around a lot. Even when they are chewing their food, they are checking to see if danger is near.

By nature, giraffes are gentle. They do not attack unless they are in danger. A giraffe will lower its head when it is angry. It will open its nostrils and its mouth. Then watch out!

Across:

2. How a giraffe feels when it lowers its head and opens its nose and mouth

4. Giraffes look this way because they are always paying attention.

6. By nature, giraffes are _____.

7. The continent where giraffes live

9. Another name for a black giraffe is

_____.

Down:

1. The patterns of a giraffe's spots

3. An animal's ability to blend with surroundings is called protective _____.

5. _____ means a certain kind of animal.

8. Giraffes' eyes are so keen they can see another animal a mile _____.

10. Are giraffes often mean?

Name: _____

Recognizing Details: Giraffes

Directions: Review what you learned about giraffes. Then answer the questions.

1. How are a giraffe's spots helpful? _____

_____

2. Is it easy to sneak up on a giraffe? Why not? _____

_____

3. What makes a giraffe look so gentle? _____

_____

4. How do you know when a giraffe is angry? _____

_____

5. Do you think a giraffe in a zoo is as observant as a giraffe in the wilds of Africa? Why or why not?

_____

_____

6. Do you think giraffes have any other enemies besides lions? _____

What animals might they be? _____

_____

7. Why do you suppose giraffes grow so large? _____

_____

8. Use a dictionary. What does **habitat** mean? Describe the giraffe's natural habitat.

_____

_____

_____

Name: _____

Comprehension: Wild Horses

Directions: Read about wild horses. Then answer the questions.

Have you ever heard of a car called a Mustang? It is named after a type of wild horse.

In the 1600s, the Spanish explorers who came to North America brought horses with them. Some of these horses escaped onto the prairies and plains. With no one to feed them or ride them, they became wild. Their numbers quickly grew, and they roamed in herds. They ran free and ate grass on the prairie.

Later, when the West was settled, people needed horses. They captured wild ones. This was not easy to do. Wild horses could run very fast. They did not want to be captured!

Some men made their living by capturing wild horses, taming them and selling them. These men were called "mustangers." Can you guess why?

After cars were invented, people did not need as many horses. Not as many mustangers were needed to catch them. More and more wild horses roamed the western prairies. In 1925, about a million mustangs were running loose.

The government was worried that the herds would eat too much grass. Ranchers who owned big herds of cattle complained that their animals didn't have enough to eat because the mustangs ate all the grass. Permission was given to ranchers and others to kill many of the horses. Thousands were killed and sold to companies that made them into pet food.

Now, wild horses live in only 12 states. The largest herds are in California, New Mexico, Oregon, Wyoming and Nevada. Most people who live in these states never see wild horses. The herds live away from people in the distant plains and mountains. They are safer there.

1. What is one type of wild horse called?_____

2. What were men called who captured wild horses?_____

3. About how many wild horses were running free in the U.S. in 1925? _____

4. The wild mustangs were killed and turned into ☐ cars. ☐ pet food. ☐ lunch meat.

5. The largest herds of wild horses are now in

☐ Oregon.   ☐ Ohio.   ☐ New Mexico.   ☐ Wyoming.

☐ California.   ☐ Nevada.   ☐ Kansas.   ☐ Arkansas.

Main Idea: More About Wild Horses

Directions: Read more about wild horses. Then answer the questions.

Have you noticed that in any large group, one person seems to be the leader? This is true for wild horses, too. The leader of a band of wild horses is a stallion. Stallions are adult male horses.

The stallion's job is important. He watches out for danger. If a bear or other animal comes close, he lets out a warning cry. This helps keep the other horses safe. Sometimes they all run away together. Other times, the stallion protects the other horses. He shows his teeth. He rears up on his back legs. Often, he scares the other animal away. Then the horses can safely continue eating grass.

Much of the grass on the prairies is gone now. Wild horses must move around a lot to find new grass. They spend about half their time eating and looking for food. If they cannot find prairie grass, wild horses will eat tree bark. They will eat flowers. If they can't find these either, wild horses will eat anything that grows!

Wild horses also need plenty of water. It is often hot in the places where they roam. At least twice a day, they find streams and take long, long drinks. Like people, wild horses lose water when they sweat. They run and sweat a lot in hot weather. To survive, they need as much water as they can get.

Wild horses also use water another way. When they find deep water, they wade into it. It feels good! It cools their skin.

1. What is the main idea? (Check one.)

_____ Wild horses need plenty of water.

_____ Wild horses move in bands protected by a stallion.

_____ Wild horses eat grass.

2. What are two reasons why wild horses need water? _____

_____

3. Why do wild horses move around so much? _____

4. What do wild horses most like to eat? _____

5. What do wild horses spend half their time doing? _____

_____

Recognizing Details: Wild Horses

Directions: Review what you read about wild horses. Then answer the questions.

1. How did horses come to North America and become wild? _____

_____

2. Why is it so difficult to capture, tame and train wild horses? _____

_____

3. Do you think it was right of the government to allow the killing of wild horses? _____

   Explain your answer. _____

_____

4. Do you think the remaining wild horses should be protected? _____

   Explain your answer. _____

_____

5. What is the role of the lead stallion in a wild horse herd? _____

_____

6. What are some things wild horses have in common with giraffes? _____

_____

_____

_____

7. What do you think will happen to wild horses as the prairie lands continue to disappear as a result of developments for homes and businesses?

_____

_____

_____

Name: _____

Comprehension: Sea Lions

Directions: Read about sea lions. Then answer the questions.

Sea lions are friendly-looking animals. Their round faces and whiskers remind people of the faces of small dogs. The almond shape of their eyes gives them a look of intelligence. Whether it is true or not, sea lions often look as though they are thinking.

Sea lions behave like playful children. They push each other off rocks. They slide into the water. Sometimes they body surf! Like people, they often ride the crest of waves. They let the waves carry them near the shore. Then they swim back out to ride more waves.

Although sea lions do not have real toys, they like to play with seaweed. They toss it in the air. They catch it in their mouths. Yuck! They must not mind the taste!

If you have been to a marine park, you may have watched sea lions. Sea lions can be taught many tricks. They can balance balls on their noses. They can jump through hoops. Their trainers give them fish to reward them for doing tricks. Sea lions look very pleased with themselves when they perform. They love fish, and they grow to love applause.

1. What are three ways sea lions play? _____

_____

_____

_____

2. Why do sea lions look intelligent? _____

_____

3. What tricks can sea lions be taught to do? _____

_____

4. As a reward, trainers give sea lions

☐ fish.   ☐ hugs.   ☐ applause.

Recognizing Details: More About Sea Lions

Directions: Read more about sea lions. Then answer the questions.

Sea lions love water! That is a good thing, because they spend most of their lives in it. Usually, the water is very cold. People cannot stay in cold water very long. The coldness slows down a person's heartbeat. It can actually make a person's heart stop beating.

Sea lions do not feel the cold. Their bodies are covered with a special layer of fat called blubber. The blubber is like a thick coat. It keeps the sea lion's body heat in. It keeps the bone-chilling cold out.

Like people, sea lions are mammals. They have warm blood. They breathe air. Baby sea lions are born on land. The mother sea lions produce milk for their babies. Like human babies, sea lions snuggle up with their mothers when they nurse. The mother knows just what her baby smells like. This is how she tells which baby is hers. She will only nurse her own baby.

Baby sea lions are called pups. Female sea lions are called cows. Male sea lions are called bulls. When pups are a few days old, their mothers leave them for a while each day. They go into the ocean to hunt fish. The pups don't seem to mind. They gather together in small groups called pods. The pods are like a nursery school! But no teacher is in charge. As many as 200 pups may spend the day together playing, swimming and sleeping.

1. What are male, female and baby sea lions called? _____

_____

2. How do sea lions stay warm in cold water? _____

_____

3. When do cows begin to leave their pups? _____

4. Where do the cows go? _____

5. What are small groups of pups called? _____

6. How can a cow tell which pup is hers? _____

Name: _____

Main Idea: Pupping Time

Directions: Read about sea lion "pupping time." Then answer the questions.

When sea lion cows gather on the beach to give birth, it is called "pupping time." Pupping time is never a surprise. It always occurs in June. Thousands of sea lions may gather in one spot for pupping time. It is sort of like one big birthday party.

The cow stays with her pups for about a week after birth. During that time, she never leaves her baby. If she must go somewhere, she drags her pup along. She grabs the loose skin around her pup's neck with her teeth. To humans, it doesn't look comfortable, but it doesn't hurt the pup.

One place the mother must go is to the water. Because of her blubber, she gets hot on land. To cool off, she takes a dip in the ocean. When she comes out, she sniffs her pup to make sure she's got the right baby. Then she drags him back again to a spot she has staked out. After a week of being dragged around, do you think the pup is ready to play?

1. Why do thousands of sea lions gather together at a certain time? _____

_____

2. Why isn't pupping time ever a surprise? _____

_____

3. How does a cow take her pup along when she goes for a cool dip?

First, grab _____.

Then, _____.

After the swim, sniff _____.

4. What is the main idea? (Check one.)

_____ Thousands of cows gather at pupping time to give birth and afterwards stay with their pups for a week.

_____ Thousands of sea lions take cools dips and usually drag their pups along.

_____ Pups are born in June.

Name: _____

Comprehension: Sea Lions

Directions: Review what you read about sea lions. Then answer the questions.

1. What makes sea lions so friendly looking? _____

_____

2. How are people like sea lions? _____

_____

_____

3. Pretend you are a pup in a pod. What would your day be like? What would you do? What would you play?

_____

_____

_____

_____

4. Why do sea lions go into the water so much? _____

_____

5. How do you think sea lions protect themselves? _____

_____

6. What is the sea lion's habitat like? _____

_____

_____

_____

_____

Review

Directions: Follow the instructions. Write your answers.

1. Create a wild animal alphabet and illustrate it on drawing paper.

   Example: A — ALLIGATOR

   B — BEAR

   C — CROCODILE

2. Select one of the wild animals you read about. Make a diorama of its habitat. A **diorama** is a three-dimensional model of a scene.

3. Compare the giraffe, wild horse and sea lion. List the ways the three animals are alike and the ways they are different.

	Giraffe	Wild Horses	Seal Lions
Alike	_____	_____	_____
Different	_____	_____	_____

4. What physical characteristics of the three animals help them survive. Which do you think is the best and why?

   _____

   _____

   _____

5. How do these animal stories differ from the animal legends and fables you read?

   _____

   _____

   _____

   _____

Name: _____

Recognizing Details: Pet Rabbits

Directions: Read about pet rabbits. Then answer the questions.

Rabbits come in many colors, and their fur has many patterns. The Dutch rabbit has white in the front of its body and brown on the back. Its ears are brown, too, and it has a brown "mask" over its eyes. Its front legs are white and its back legs are brown. The tips of the toes on its back legs are white.

People think Dutch rabbits are adorable! They look like stuffed toys and weigh about five pounds when fully grown. The rabbit is called "Dutch," but it was first bred in Belgium.

Another popular rabbit is the Californian. Can you guess where it was first bred? It is a fat white rabbit with pink eyes. The Californian rabbit has touches of light brown on its toes and nose. Its ears are light brown also.

Did you know some people raise rabbits for their fur? The fur from the Angora rabbit is actually called wool. There are 13 colors of Angora rabbit, but white is the most popular. This rabbit has long hair and pink eyes. It can grow to weigh six pounds. Because its fur is long, it must be groomed every day. To "groom" an animal means to comb and care for its fur.

Some breeds of rabbits are called giants. Compared to other rabbits, they really are big. The Belgian hare, a reddish-colored rabbit, can weigh up to 9 pounds. Other breeds are called dwarfs. Dwarfs are very small. Fully grown, they weigh only about 2 pounds. A popular dwarf rabbit is the Netherland. Most Netherland rabbits are white with pink eyes.

1. How many breeds of rabbits are named in the article? _____

2. What are the names of the breeds? _____

_____

3. What is one type of giant rabbit? _____

4. What is one type of dwarf rabbit? _____

5. How much does a Belgian hare weigh? _____

6. How much does a Dutch rabbit weigh? _____

7. Use a reference source. What is the difference between a hare and a rabbit?

_____

_____

Name: _____

Comprehension: Caring for Pet Rabbits

Directions: Read about caring for pet rabbits. Then answer the questions.

Most pet rabbits live outside in special homes, called hutches. Rabbit hutches are small and have wire on the sides and bottom to let air in. The wire on the bottom also lets the animals' droppings fall through. This helps keep their hutch clean.

Pet rabbits need exercise, too. They do not like being caged all the time. Would you? That is why pet owners build "rabbit runs" for their pets. Rabbit runs are much bigger and longer than cages. They do not have floors. They fit over the grass. Put the rabbit inside the run and guess what it does?

Some people let their rabbits run free for exercise. But you must take care that the rabbit does not run away. Only let the rabbit free if your yard is fenced. Also, you need to protect your pet from dogs and other animals.

Of course, you should pet your rabbit. To pick it up, put one hand on the back of the rabbit's neck. This area of loose skin is called the "scruff." Put your other hand under the rabbit's rear end. Then lift the rabbit slowly and firmly. Rabbits do not like fast movements. That's why you should never grab your rabbit. Also, never, never pick up your rabbit by its ears.

Hold your rabbit close to your chest. This makes the rabbit feel secure. It also keeps it from falling. Put your hand under its back legs. Hold the legs firmly so your rabbit cannot kick. Then gently scratch its fur. Rabbits cannot purr, but you can tell when your pet is happy.

1. What do pet owners build for their rabbits to exercise in? _____

2. What is the difference between a hutch and a rabbit run? _____

_____

3. What is the rabbit's "scruff"? _____

4. Never pick your rabbit up by its

☐ scruff.   ☐ ears.   ☐ body.

5. After you pick up your rabbit, hold it close to your

☐ chest.   ☐ face.   ☐ arms.

6. Hold your rabbit's legs firmly so it cannot

☐ purr.   ☐ cry.   ☐ kick.

Name: _____

Following Directions: Rabbit Food

Directions: Read about what rabbits eat. Then work the puzzle.

Many people think rabbits only eat lettuce. They do like lettuce, but it's not the only thing rabbits eat.

Rabbits also need protein. Most pet owners supply this with dry rabbit food. The food is called pellets. Rabbits should eat twice a day. They also need fresh water every day. Besides lettuce, they like carrots, cabbage and turnips. These vegetables are called greens. Rabbits like them mixed together.

Pet rabbits will eat wild plants. They like dandelion leaves and blackberry leaves. They also like a kind of plant called chickweed. Learn what these plants look like. Then pick them for your rabbit. Some plants are poisonous. For example, buttercups can kill rabbits. So can poppy flowers. If you gather wild plants, be very careful.

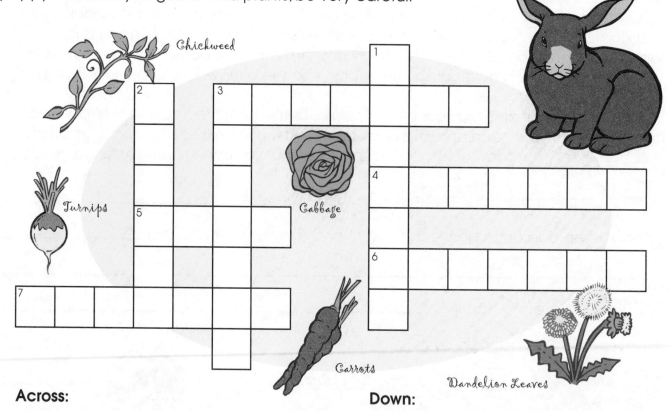

Across:

3. Pet owners feed their rabbits this in pellets.

4. A vegetable pet rabbits will eat

5. Rabbits also will eat _____ plants.

6. This vegetable is like lettuce. Rabbits like it.

7. Another vegetable rabbits like

Down:

1. Rabbits like this, but it is not the only food they like.

2. A plant that will poison a rabbit is the poppy _____.

3. Pet rabbits get their protein in these.

Name: _____

Comprehension: Baby Rabbits

Directions: Read about baby rabbits. Then answer the questions.

Many people think newborn animals are cute. Baby rabbits grow inside their mothers for only 31 days before they are born. They complete a lot of their development outside the mother. When they are born, they have no fur. They look like little rats! Would you call newborn rabbits cute?

The babies are blind, and they don't open their eyes until they are 10 days old. At the beginning, they can only feel their mother. They cannot see her.

When they are first born, baby rabbits are very delicate. It could hurt them if you picked them up. Do not touch them until they are at least 3 weeks old. By then, they will have fur. Their eyes will be open. Their ears will be standing up. They will finally look like rabbits!

Even though they are much stronger after three weeks, do not hold them long. Their mother will not like it. Like most mothers, she feels a strong need to protect her babies. Also, they are still nursing. This means they are drinking her milk. They need her milk to grow stronger, and they need it often. That is why you should not hold the babies very long.

By the time they are 6 weeks old, baby rabbits are active. They can eat food other than their mother's milk. When they are 8 weeks old, you can move them into their own hutch. They do not need their mother anymore to survive. They are still growing, though. Adult rabbits need only two meals a day. Baby rabbits need three meals a day until they are 3 months old.

1. How long does the baby rabbit grow inside the mother? _____

2. When do baby rabbits open their eyes? _____

3. Why is it unwise to handle newborn rabbits? _____

_____

4. Baby rabbits are active by the time they have lived how many weeks? _____

5. You can pick up baby rabbits when they are how many weeks old? _____

6. Baby rabbits can move into their own hutch when they are how many weeks old? _____

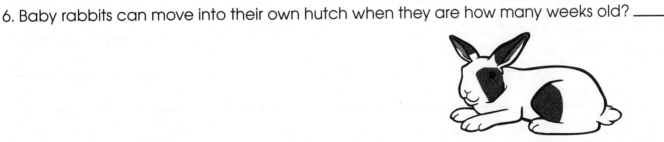

Name: _____

Comprehension: Rabbits

Directions: Review what you learned about rabbits as pets. Then answer the questions.

1. How do baby rabbits look when they are first born? _____

_____

2. Discuss uses of rabbit fur, especially Angora. _____

_____

3. Angora wool comes in 13 colors. What do you think they are? _____

_____

_____

4. Why do many people think rabbits are cute? _____

_____

5. The article mentioned several reasons why you need to be extremely careful with a baby rabbit. Write an explanation for each one.

_____

_____

_____

_____

6. What makes a rabbit feel secure? _____

_____

_____

7. Would you like a pet rabbit? _____ Why or why not? _____

_____

_____

_____

Main Idea: Pet Snakes

Directions: Read about pet snakes. Then answer the questions.

Having a snake for a pet is considered very strange by some people! Snakes can be good pets. They are not cuddly like kittens. Like fish, snakes are interesting to watch.

Many people are afraid of snakes. They do not know much about them. One important fact about snakes is that most of them are not poisonous. Only four types of poisonous snakes live in the United States.

People who keep snakes as pets usually put them in cages. The snake must fit comfortably inside. Many snake owners put their pets in empty fish tanks. The snakes like the smooth glass. The owner can see exactly what the snake is doing. You can also put a snake in a wooden cage, but make sure the wood is sanded smooth. Otherwise, it can hurt the snake's skin.

You need to line a snake's cage with newspaper or sand. You will need to change the bedding two or three times each week.

Snakes like privacy. Put a large rock inside your pet's cage. The snake will coil around it. A large log is also good "snake furniture." The snake will crawl up on its "sofa" when it wants to relax.

Some snakes like to wet their skins. Put a big bowl of water in the cage. The bowl should be heavy so the snake can't tip it over. Then the snake can get into its bowl and soak for a while. This makes a good bath for a snake!

1. What is the main idea? (Check one.)

_____ Many people are afraid of snakes, but they shouldn't be afraid.
There are only four kinds of poisonous snakes in the United States.

_____ Snakes like to crawl.

_____ Snakes are interesting to watch and can make good pets for certain people. Like other pets, they require care.

2. Why do snakes make good pets for some people? _____

_____

3. Why should you put a rock inside a pet snake's cage? _____

_____

4. How often should you change the bedding in a pet snake's cage? _____

Main Idea: Snakes

Directions: Read about snakes. Then answer the questions.

Snakes are **reptiles**. This means they are cold-blooded (their body temperture changes with the surrounding temperature), they lay eggs and their bodies are covered with scales. Many people think the scales are slimey, but they're not. Snakes have smooth, dry skin.

When baby snakes hatch, they are very small. They eat insects and worms. Some kinds of snakes never get very big, and they eat insects and worms all of their lives. Some kinds of snakes, however, can get quite large. The python in Africa can grow to be more than 20 feet long!

Bigger snakes need to eat bigger food. These snakes eat animals like mice, rats or even rabbits and frogs. Some farmers like to see snakes around their barns because snakes eat the rodents that get into the grain.

When snakes grow, their skin doesn't grow with them. They have to shed their skin. The old skin loosens up all over the snake's body, and the snake rubs against rough surfaces like trees and rocks to make it come off. During this time, the snake is blind. If you have a pet snake that is shedding, watch out! Since it can't see, it might think your hand is food and try to bite it. It is best to leave snakes alone when they are shedding. When the snake is done shedding, it can see again, and it has a nice new skin.

1. What is the main idea? (Check one.)

_____ Different snakes eat different kinds of foods, but they all shed their skins as they grow.

_____ Snakes eat insects and worms after they hatch.

_____ Farmers like snakes because they shed their skins.

2. What is a reptile? _____

_____

3. How big can some snakes grow to be? _____

4. Using context clues, write the definition of the word **rodent**? _____

_____

_____

Name: _____

Recognizing Details: Snakes

Directions: Review what you learned about snakes. Then answer the questions.

1. Why is having a pet snake considered strange? _____

_____

2. Do you agree with this? Why or why not? _____

_____

3. Are you afraid of snakes? Explain your answer. _____

_____

_____

4. How is caring for a rabbit like caring for a snake? _____

_____

_____

5. How is it different? _____

_____

_____

6. How do snakes shed their skins? _____

_____

_____

7. What does "cold-blooded" mean? _____

_____

_____

8. What are some other animals that are cold-blooded? _____

_____

Review

Directions: Review what you learned about animals as pets. Then answer the questions.

1. What other types of animals are common pets? _____

_____

2. Do the animals listed in your answer above require much care? _____

Explain. _____

_____

_____

3. Do you have a pet? _____ What is it? _____

Explain how you care for it. _____

_____

_____

4. If you do not have a pet, write a short paragraph to your parents convincing them you could care for one.

_____

_____

_____

_____

5. What animal do you think makes the best pet? _____

Explain. _____

_____

_____

_____

Name: _____

Recognizing Details: Going to Camp

Directions: Read about going to camp. Then answer the questions.

Have you ever gone to camp? If so, you know you need to pack many things. Usually, the people who run the camp will send a list of what you need to bring. What you need depends on the type of camp and how long you will stay.

If you go to camp for one week, you will probably need the following items. Pack them all in a suitcase or gym bag—if they will fit!

1 bathing suit	5 pairs of shorts	1 pair of sneakers
2 sweaters or sweatshirts	1 jacket	2 pairs of jeans
7 pairs of underwear	2 towels	1 washcloth
1 brush and comb	1 bottle of shampoo	1 bar of soap
1 bottle of sunscreen	1 bottle of insect spray	1 flashlight
1 toothbrush and tube of toothpaste	7 short-sleeve shirts	

There are many kinds of camps. There are church camps and scout camps. There are horseback-riding camps, swimming camps, music camps and nature camps. There are sports camps and cheerleading camps. There are even camps for losing weight!

Some city children take a bus to camp. The bus picks up a whole group of children and takes them to the country. Other children are taken to camp by their parents. Their parents look at their cabins. They sit on the bunk beds and say, "This feels comfortable." They look at the camp menu and say, "The food looks good." Then they say, "Good-bye. Have fun. Be careful. See you in a week!"

1. How many pairs of underwear do you need for a week at camp? _____

2. How many pairs of shorts should you bring? _____

3. How many things on the list do you need only one of? _____

4. What are two things you could put your clothes in? _____

_____

5. Is there anything not listed that you think you would need at camp? What? _____

_____

6. If you were going to a football camp, what else might you need to bring along?

_____

Comprehension: Camping Out

Directions: Read about camping out. Then answer the questions.

Going away to camp and camping out are two very different experiences. Usually, children who go to camp sleep on cots inside cabins. Activities are planned by the people who run the camp. Campers eat in a dining hall. The food is prepared by someone else. All the campers have to do is show up and complain about what's being served!

When you camp out, the experience is much more rugged. You sleep in a tent instead of a cabin. If it's warm, you may unroll your sleeping bag under the stars. To camp out, you must be much more independent. You must learn certain skills, such as how to pitch a tent and how to start a fire. You need to know some rules about safety and respecting the outdoors. You may even need to know how to catch and cook your own food!

The Boy Scouts teach their members an "outdoor code" before they camp. It is a good code for any camper to follow. Here is a summary of the Boy Scouts' Outdoor Code:

"I will treat the outdoors as a heritage to be improved for greater enjoyment. I will keep my trash out of America's fields, woods and roadways. I will prevent wildfires. I will build my fire in a safe place and be sure it is out when I leave.

Use of the outdoors is a privilege I can lose by abuse. I will treat the environment with respect. I will learn to practice good conservation of soil, water, forests and wildlife, and I will urge others to do the same."

1. What are two of the things you need to know about before camping out?

_____

_____

2. What is the name of the camping rules the Boy Scouts are taught to follow?

_____

3. What is one way Boy Scouts show they will treat the outdoors as a heritage to be improved?

_____

_____

4. What is one way camping out is different from going away to camp?

_____

Following Directions: Campfires

Directions: Read about building campfires. Then work the puzzle.

Where there is fire, there is always danger. That is why only people who know exactly what they are doing should build a campfire. Many campsites do not allow campfires. Campers bring portable cook stoves to these sites.

Sites that do allow campfires often provide firelays. A firelay is a 10-foot-round cleared area. In the area there may be a grill, metal ring or outdoor stone fireplace. These firelays are safe because they keep the fire contained in a small area. Firelays help keep cooking fires from spreading and turning into wildfires.

Across:

2. This is hot and always dangerous.

3. The shape of a firelay

4. When campfires are not allowed, use a ____ stove.

5. A ____ ring is sometimes found in a firelay.

7. Sometimes a ____ fireplace is provided in the firelay.

Down:

1. The purpose of a firelay is to make sure a fire doesn't ____ .

2. 10-foot-round circles for building campfires

6. A firelay keeps the fire contained in a small ____ .

Comprehension: First-Aid Kits

Directions: Read about first-aid kits. Then answer the questions.

Something you should be sure to take when you camp is a first-aid kit. Cuts, scrapes and insect bites or stings all can happen when camping. You must also be prepared for accidental poisoning. What if someone eats a berry that is poisonous? You will need to get the poison out of his/her system right away!

First-aid kits will help you in an emergency. Here are some things that go into a well-packed first-aid kit:

1 small bottle of ipecac syrup (Ipecac causes vomiting. It will immediately clear poison from the body.)

1 thermometer to check for fever

1 bottle of aspirin to hold down fever and ease pain

1 unopened bar of soap to wash cuts and scrapes

1 box of sterile bandages, adhesive tape and gauze pads for covering wounds after they have been cleaned

1 large triangular bandage to make a sling for an injured or broken arm

1 pair of tweezers to pull out splinters or bee stingers

1 bottle of calamine lotion to treat poison ivy and insect bites

1 bag of sterile cotton balls to clean cuts

1 eyecup and sterile water to wash out injured eyes

Many people keep first-aid kits in their cars. Then, if an emergency happens when they travel, they are always prepared. Does your family have a first-aid kit?

1. Why is a first-aid kit important when camping? _____

_____

2. What items in your first-aid kit would you use to treat these conditions?

A scrape? _____

A fever? _____

A sprained arm? _____

3. When would you give someone ipecac syrup? _____

_____

Main Idea: Choosing a Campsite

Directions: Read about choosing a campsite. Then answer the questions.

If you are camping at a campground, you will not have much choice about where you camp. You must stay within the site area the owners show you. If you are camping in the wilderness, you can choose your own campsite.

A good campsite will have water nearby for drinking and cooking. Look for ground that is level and dry. Avoid rocky ground, or you will be uncomfortable when you try to sleep. If you plan to build a fire, look for dry firewood to gather nearby.

You will also need to be on the lookout for things you do not want. Hornets' nests, poison ivy and anthills can make your camping trip miserable. If you see any nearby, set up your campsite elsewhere. You will also want to avoid camping near bears or other animals. If you see animal tracks, take them as a sign that animals have already "staked out" the area. For your own safety, move on.

It's important when camping in the wilderness to let someone know where you are. Otherwise, if you get lost, no one will know! Then who would come to rescue you? Find the park rangers' station when you go into any wilderness area and talk to the rangers. It is their job to know the forest. They can tell you about which places to seek out and which to avoid.

A good plan is to promise to stop by after your trip. That way, they will know you returned safely. If you do not show up, they will come looking for you. Taking these few practical precautions will make your trip safer and more fun.

1. What is the main idea? (Check one.)

_____ Picking a good campsite and checking in with park rangers will help to make your wilderness camping trip a safe and enjoyable experience.

_____ Avoiding poison ivy and anthills are the most important things you can do to make your wilderness trip a safe one.

_____ Watch out for bears when you go camping.

2. Why should you tell park rangers where you will be? (Check one.)

_____ They can bring messages to you if there is an emergency at home.

_____ They can send searchers to look for you if you do not return.

_____ They can stop by for a cup of coffee if they get lonely.

Comprehension: Time to Eat!

Directions: Read about what to eat on a camping trip. Then answer the questions.

A wilderness camping trip will make you appreciate your kitchen, your bathroom, your bed and your comfortable living room furniture.

Food and water are among the most important things to bring on a camping trip. Remember, you will have to carry everything you need on your back. That's why it's smart to bring things that don't weigh too much. Because they are light, dried food and powdered drinks are good things for campers to bring. Then the campers add sterilized water to them and—presto!—a meal!

Many campers pack these foods: dry cereal, dried fruit, powdered eggs, raisins, dried potatoes, dried soup, powdered milk, instant cocoa, dried meat or dried chicken and rice.

The total weight of all the food listed is under four pounds. Even a tired camper can carry four pounds easily. Imagine if you had to carry a gallon of milk, a couple of whole chickens, a roast, a bag of red potatoes and a dozen eggs! It would certainly weigh a lot more. Besides, the eggs would probably get broken, and the milk would get sour.

The best thing most people can say about dried food is that it's "not bad." If you have ever eaten it, you know that fresh, whole food tastes better. But the sights and sounds of camping in the wilderness make up for the dried food. If you are lucky, you will work up such an appetite hiking that even dried food will taste great!

1. Why do campers take along dried and powdered food? _____

_____

2. What is the best thing most people can say about dried food?

_____

3. What are five kinds of dried food? _____

_____

4. What is the total weight of all the dried food listed in the article? _____

Recognizing Details: Three Kinds of Tents

Directions: Read about tents. Then answer the questions.

Tarp Tent

The tarp tent is the simplest tent. It is called a "one-man" tent because only one person will fit inside. Tarp tents have no floors. They have no windows or doors. They do not have netting. To put one up, you need to find a tree to hook one corner to.

Pup Tent

Two people can sleep in a pup tent. Some pup tents come with attached floors. They do not have windows. Like the tarp tent, the front of a pup tent is open. Pup tents have no doors.

Umbrella Tent

Umbrella tents are larger than pup tents or tarp tents. This means more people can sleep inside. They have floors and a door. Some have windows. The doors and windows can be left open. Netting can be pulled across the front of the doors and windows. The netting lets in air and keeps out bugs.

1. Which tents have no doors or windows? _____

2. Which tent needs to be pitched near a tree? _____

3. Which tent has no floor? _____

4. Which tent has netting to keep out bugs? _____

5. Which tent sleeps only one person? _____

6. Which tent can two people sleep in? _____

Recognizing Details: Getting Lost

Directions: Read about what to do if you get lost in the woods. Then answer the questions.

Even experienced campers sometimes get lost. To avoid getting lost, stay on marked trails. Take a notepad and pencil with you for jotting notes. Use a compass so you know what direction you are going. To find your way with a compass, you must know which way you want to go. Before you leave your camp, find a large landmark nearby to mark your campsite. Head in the opposite direction from the landmark. If your compass shows you are going west, which direction will you travel to return to your campsite? East.

If you do get lost, don't panic. This is the worst thing you can do. People who panic have been known to walk in big circles. They don't realize this, of course. They exhaust themselves and never get back on course.

If it is late, and others know you are out hiking, stay where you are. Someone will come looking for you soon.

If it is early, and you want to try to find your way back, leave trail markers to show you where you have been. Tie a handkerchief to a branch. Put a pile of stones on the trail you have taken. If you have a pen and notepad in your pack, write a note and put it on a tree. Write down the time, date, the fact that you are lost and the direction you are now hiking.

If you are lost at night, build two campfires close together. Two columns of smoke side by side are a signal for help. Rangers and campers will recognize and respond to the fires. They will locate your smoke signals and come to find you.

In the meantime, use extra clothes from your pack to stay warm. Be patient and wait until help arrives.

1. Complete the directions on what to do if you get lost in the woods.

   Tie a _____ .

   Put a pile _____ .

   If you have a pen and notepad, _____ .

   If you are lost at night, build _____ .

2. What is the main idea? (Check one.)

   _____ It is nearly impossible to get lost while hiking.

   _____ If you get lost, use a compass to find your way back.

   _____ Avoid panicking if you get lost by following some simple steps.

Name: _____

Review

Directions: Review what you learned about camping. Then answer the questions.

1. What items should you take on a camping trip? _____

_____

2. Of the items you wrote, circle the two you feel are the most important.

3. Why is it important to carry camping gear and food that is light in weight?

_____

4. What should you look for when selecting a campsite? _____

_____

5. What would you not want near your site? _____

_____

6. What are the safety reasons for finding a park rangers' station and talking to the rangers?

_____

_____

7. What can you do to avoid getting lost? _____

_____

8. What should you do if you do get lost? _____

_____

9. Have you ever been camping? Explain your experience. _____

_____

If not, describe what you think it would be like to go camping. _____

_____

Name: _____

Sequencing: "Mr. Nobody"

Directions: After reading the poem "Mr. Nobody," number in order the things people blame him for.

I know a funny little man
As quiet as a mouse,
Who does the mischief that is done
In everybody's house!
No one ever sees his face.
And yet we all agree
That every plate we break was cracked
By Mr. Nobody.

It's he who always tears out books,
Who leaves the door ajar,
He pulls the buttons from our shirts,
And scatters pins afar;
That squeaking door will always squeak,
The reason is, you see,
We leave the oiling to be done
By Mr. Nobody.

The finger marks upon the wall
By none of us are made;
We never leave the blinds unclosed
To let the carpet fade.
The bowl of soup we do not spill,
It's not our fault, you see
These mishaps—every one is caused
By Mr. Nobody.

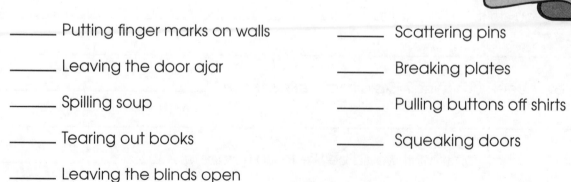

_____ Putting finger marks on walls

_____ Leaving the door ajar

_____ Spilling soup

_____ Tearing out books

_____ Leaving the blinds open

_____ Scattering pins

_____ Breaking plates

_____ Pulling buttons off shirts

_____ Squeaking doors

Name: _____

Comprehension: "The Chickens"

Directions: Read the poem "The Chickens." Then answer the questions.

Said the first little chicken
With a queer little squirm,
"I wish I could find
A fat little worm!"

Said the next little chicken
With an odd little shrug.
"I wish I could find
A fat little bug!"

Said the third little chicken
With a small sigh of grief,
"I wish I could find
A green little leaf!"

Said the fourth little chicken
With a faint little moan,
"I wish I could find
A small gravel stone!"

"See here!" said the mother
From the green garden patch,
"If you want any breakfast,
Just come here and scratch!"

1. What does the second little chicken want? _____

2. Which meal are all the chickens wishing for? _____

3. Where is the mother hen? _____

4. Which of the following do the chickens not want?

_____ leaf   _____ corn   _____ worm   _____ bug   _____ stone

5. What does the mother hen tell her chicks to do if they want breakfast?

_____

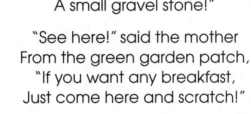

Name: _____

Following Directions: "I'm Glad"

Directions: Read the poem "I'm Glad." Then work the puzzle.

I'm glad the sky is painted blue
And the Earth is painted green,
With such a lot of nice fresh air
All sandwiched in between.

Across:

3. The sky is painted this color.

4. How what we breathe is placed between the Earth and sky

6. This is what we breathe, and it's between the Earth and sky.

Down:

1. The color of the Earth in the poem

2. How the speaker feels

4. Painted blue

5. Painted green

Comprehension: "Over the Hills and Far Away"

Directions: Read "Over the Hills and Far Away." Then answer the questions.

Tom, Tom the piper's son,
Learned to play when he was one,
But the only tune that he could play
Was "Over the Hills and Far Away."

Now Tom with his pipe made such a noise
That he pleased the girls and he pleased the boys,
And they all danced when they heard him play
"Over the Hills and Far Away."

Tom played his pipe with such great skill,
Even pigs and dogs could not keep still.
The dogs would wag their tails and dance,
The pigs would oink and grunt and prance.

Yes, Tom could play, his music soared—
But soon the pigs and dogs got bored.
The children, too, thought it was wrong,
For Tom to play just one dull song.

1. How old is Tom when he learns to play? _____

2. What tune does Tom play? _____

_____

3. What do the dogs do when Tom plays? _____

_____

4. Why does everyone get tired of Tom's music? _____

_____

5. What do the pigs do when Tom plays? _____

_____

6. What instrument does Tom play? _____

Sequencing: "The Spider and the Fly"

Directions: Read the poem "The Spider and the Fly." Then number the events in order.

"Won't you come into my parlor?" said the spider to the fly.
"It's the nicest little parlor that you will ever spy.
The way into my parlor is up a winding stair.
I have so many pretty things to show you inside there."

The little fly said, "No! No! No! To do so is not sane.
For those who travel up your stair do not come down again."

The spider turned himself around and went back in his den –
He knew for sure the silly fly would visit him again.
The spider wove a tiny web, for he was very sly
He was making preparations to trap the silly fly.

Then out his door the spider came and merrily did sing,
"Oh, fly, oh lovely, lovely fly with pearl and silver wings."

Alas! How quickly did the fly come buzzing back to hear
The spider's words of flattery, which drew the fly quite near.

The fly was trapped within the web, the spider's winding stair,
Then the spider jumped upon him, and ate the fly right there!

_____ The spider sings a song about how beautiful the fly is.

_____ The spider jumps on the fly.

_____ The spider invites the fly into his parlor.

_____ The spider spins a tiny new web to catch the fly.

_____ The fly becomes caught in the spider's web.

_____ The fly says he knows it's dangerous to go into the spider's parlor.

_____ The spider eats the fly.

_____ The fly comes near the web to hear the song.

Name: _____

Comprehension: "Grasshopper Green"

Directions: Read the poem "Grasshopper Green." Then answer the questions.

Grasshopper Green is a comical guy,
He lives on the best of fare.
Bright little trousers, jacket and cap,
These are his summer wear.

Out in the meadow he loves to go,
Playing away in the sun.
It's hopperty, skipperty, high and low,
Summer's the time for fun.

Grasshopper Green has a cute little house,
He stays near it every day.
It's under the hedge where he is safe,
Out of the gardener's way.

Gladly he's calling the children to play
Out in the beautiful sun
It's hopperty, skipperty, high and low,
Summer's the time for fun.

1. What does **comical** mean in this poem?_____

2. What are three things Grasshopper Green wears in the summer?

_____

3. Where does he love to go and play?_____

4. Whom does Grasshopper Green call to play? _____

5. What is summer the time for?_____

6. Use a dictionary. What does **fare** mean in this poem? _____

7. You won't find the words **hopperty** and **skipperty** in a dictionary. Based on the poem, write your own definitions of these words.

_____

_____

Name: _____

Main Idea: "Little Robin Redbreast"

Directions: Read the poem "Little Robin Redbreast." Then answer the questions.

Little Robin Redbreast
Sat up in a tree,
Up went the kitty cat
Down went he.

Down came the kitty cat—
Away Robin ran,
Said little Robin Redbreast,
"Catch me if you can."

Then Little Robin Redbreast
Hopped upon a wall,
Kitty cat jumped after him,
And almost had a fall.

Little Robin chirped and sang,
And what did kitty say?
Kitty cat said, "Meow!" quite loud,
And Robin flew away.

1. What is the main idea? (Check one.)

_____ The robin is smarter than the cat and a lot faster, too.

_____ When people see a robin, it means spring is near.

_____ The robin is scared away.

2. What nearly happens when the cat jumps on the wall?

_____

3. Where is the robin when the cat first goes after him? _____

4. Where does the robin go after the cat climbs the tree? _____

5. What does the robin say to the cat? _____

Sequencing: "Hickory, Dickory, Dock"

Directions: Read the poem "Hickory, Dickory, Dock." Then answer the questions.

Hickory, dickory, dock,
The mouse ran up the clock.
The clock struck one,
And down he run,
Hickory, dickory, dock.

Dickory, dickory, dare,
The pig flew in the air.
The man in brown
Soon brought him down,
Dickory, dickory, dare.

Hickory
Dickory
Dock

1. What is the main idea? (Check one.)

_____ Mice and pigs can cause a lot of problems to clocks and men in brown suits.

_____ There is no main idea. This poem is just for fun.

_____ Beware of mice in your clocks and flying pigs.

2. Why do you think the mouse runs down the clock? _____

_____

Directions: Number these events in order.

_____ The clock strikes one.

_____ The mouse runs back down the clock.

_____ The mouse runs up the clock.

_____ The man in brown brings the pig down.

_____ The pig flies in the air.

Review

Directions: Review the poems you read. Then answer the questions.

1. How is the spider in the poem "The Spider and the Fly" like the fox in the fable "The Fox and the Crow"?

_____

_____

_____

2. Which of the poems that you read did you like the best? _____

Why? _____

_____

_____

3. Which of the poems that you read did you like the least? _____

Why? _____

_____

_____

_____

One way to remember what you read is to make a comic strip of the story or poem. Think about the poem "Mr. Nobody." Imagine what "Mr. Nobody" would look like.

Directions: Follow the sequence of events in the "Mr. Nobody" poem to make a cartoon of the poem in the boxes below

Name: _____

Review

Directions: Select one of the other poems you read. Summarize and illustrate it.

Name: _____

Recognizing Details: Earth's Atmosphere

Directions: Read about Earth's atmosphere. Then answer the questions.

The air that surrounds Earth is called the atmosphere. It surrounds Earth like a blanket—20 miles thick! The atmosphere protects Earth from the sun's heat. It helps keep heat in, too. If we had no atmosphere, the sun would fry Earth during the day. At night, it would be freezing! Earth's heat would escape into outer space. Nothing could stay alive on Earth without the atmosphere to protect us.

Did you know air can be weighed? If we could weigh the air in our atmosphere, it would weigh 6,000,000,000,000,000 (or six quadrillion) pounds. This huge figure is based on what scientists have figured out.

The air in the atmosphere is made up of dust and gases. More than three-fourths of the gas is nitrogen. Plants depend on nitrogen to stay alive. Most of the rest is made up of oxygen. Oxygen is needed for human and animal life. One percent of the atmosphere is made up of other gases. Included in this one percent are dust particles, ash from volcanoes and other bits of matter.

The gases and particles in the atmosphere are packed closer together near the ground. The farther up you go, the farther apart the gases and particles are. People who travel to the mountains find it harder to breathe the air. This is because the air is "thinner" and their lungs are not used to it. They have to work a little harder to get oxygen from this thin air. Usually, their lungs adjust quickly.

1. What are two ways the atmosphere protects Earth? _____

_____

_____

2. What gas makes up most of the atmosphere? _____

3. Where are gases and particles in the atmosphere packed closest together?

_____

4. Why is it harder to breathe in the mountains? _____

_____

5. How thick is the atmosphere? _____

Name: _____

Comprehension: Earth's Atmosphere

Directions: Review what you read about Earth's atmosphere. Then answer the questions.

1. To what does the article compare the atmosphere? _____

2. Why is air in our atmosphere so important? _____

   _____

   _____

3. How do you think thinner air in the mountains affects plant and animal life? _____

   _____

   _____

4. What do you think would happen if more of the Sun's heat would reach Earth?

   _____

5. What do you think would happen if some of the Sun's heat did not remain trapped close to Earth at night?

   _____

   _____

Scientists know that our atmosphere is continuing to thin, thus losing its ability to protect Earth from the sun's ultra-violet rays.

Directions: Use reference sources to find out more about Earth's thinning atmosphere. Select one of the topics and write a report based on your research. Include illustrations or diagrams if possible.

What is the ozone layer?

What is the Greenhouse Effect?

What caused the hole in the ozone?

What is being done about the hole in the ozone?

What is being done about the Greenhouse Effect?

What will happen if the hole in the ozone gets larger?

What will happen if the Greenhouse Effect continues?

Comprehension: Clouds

Directions: Read about clouds. Then answer the questions.

Have you ever wondered where clouds come from? Clouds are made from billions and billions of tiny water droplets in the air. The water droplets form into clouds when warm, moist air rises and is cooled.

Have you ever seen your breath when you were outside on a very cold day? Your breath is warm and moist. When it hits the cold air, it is cooled. A kind of small cloud is formed by your breath!

Clouds come in many sizes and shapes. On some days, clouds blanket the whole sky. Other times, clouds look like wispy puffs of smoke. There are other types of clouds as well.

Weather experts have named clouds. Big, fluffy clouds that look flat on the bottom are called **cumulus** clouds. **Strato-cumulus** is the name for rounded clouds that are packed very close together. You can still see patches of sky, but strato-cumulus clouds are thicker than cumulus ones.

If you spot **cumulo-nimbus** clouds, go inside. These clouds are wide at the bottom and have thin tops. The tops of these clouds are filled with ice crystals. On hot summer days, you may even have seen cumulo-nimbus clouds growing. They seem to boil and grow as though they are coming from a big pot. A violent thunderstorm usually occurs after you see these clouds. Often, there is hail.

Cumulus, strato-cumulus and cumulo-nimbus are only three of many types of clouds. If you listen closely, you will hear television weather forecasters talk about these and other clouds. Why? Because clouds are good indicators of weather.

1. How are clouds formed? _____

_____

2. How can you make your own cloud? _____

_____

3. What should you do when you spot cumulo-nimbus clouds?

_____

4. What often happens after you see cumulo-nimbus clouds? _____

_____

5. What kind of big fluffy clouds look flat on the bottom? _____

Name: _____

Recognizing Details: Clouds

Directions: Review what you learned about clouds. Then answer the questions.

1. How are clouds a good indicator of the weather? _____

_____

2. When you take something out of the freezer on a warm day, why do you think it looks like steam is rising from the object? _____

_____

3. What does this have to do with clouds? _____

_____

Directions: Use cotton balls to make models of the three types of clouds.

Name: _____

Following Directions: Rain

Directions: Read about rain. Then work the puzzle.

Rain develops from water vapor, dust and temperature inside clouds. From this combination, water droplets form and grow. When the droplets become too heavy for the cloud, they fall as rain. Weather experts say that when it storms, the raindrops are about 0.02 inches (0.5 millimeters) in size.

Sometimes the air below the rain cloud is very dry. The dry air dries out the wetness of the raindrop and turns it back into water vapor before it hits the ground. This is what happens in the summer when it looks as though it will rain but doesn't. The rain begins to fall, but it dries up before it falls all the way to the ground.

Across:

2. These form from water vapor, dust and the temperature inside clouds.

4. Falls when the water droplets become too heavy for the clouds

5. Season when the air under the cloud sometimes dries the rain before it hits the ground

Down:

1. When water droplets inside clouds get this way, rain falls.

2. Combines with water vapor and the temperature inside clouds

3. Raindrops measure about 0.02 inches (0.5 mm) when it _____.

Comprehension: Thunderstorms

Directions: Read about thunderstorms. Then answer the questions.

Thunderstorms can be scary! The sky darkens. The air feels heavy. Then the thunder begins. Sometimes the thunder sounds like a low rumble. Other times thunder is very loud. Loud thunder can be heard 15 miles away.

Thunderstorms begin inside big cumulo-nimbus clouds. Remember, cumulo-nimbus are the summer clouds that seem to boil and grow. It is as though there is a big pot under the clouds.

Thunder is heard after lightning flashes across the sky. The noise of thunder happens when lightning heats the air as it cuts through it. Some people call this quick, sharp sound a thunderclap. Sometimes thunder sounds "rumbly." This rumble is the thunder's sound wave bouncing off hills and mountains.

Weather experts say there is an easy way to figure out how far away a storm is. First, look at your watch. Count the number of seconds between the flash of lightning and the sound of thunder. To find how far away the storm is, divide the number of seconds by five. This will give the number of miles the storm is from you.

How far away is the storm if you count 20 seconds between the flash of lightning and the sound of thunder? Twenty divided by five is four miles. What if you count only five seconds? One mile! Get inside quickly. The air is charged with electricity. You could be stuck by lightning. It is not safe to be outside in a thunderstorm.

1. Where do thunderstorms begin? _____

2. When is thunder heard? _____

3. What causes thunder to sound rumbly? _____

_____

4. To find out how far away a storm is, count the seconds between the thunder and lightning and divide by what number?

_____

5. If you count 40 seconds between the lightning and thunder, how far away is the storm?

_____

6. What comes first, thunder or lightning? _____

Name: _____

Recognizing Details: Lightning Safety

Directions: Read about safety rules for lightning. Then answer the questions.

During a storm, lightning can be very dangerous. If you are outside when a thunderstorm begins, look for shelter in a building. If you are in the woods, look for a cave. If you are in an open field, lie down in a hole. If there is no hole, lie flat on the ground.

Standing in an open field, your body is like a lightning rod. Never look for shelter under a tree during a thunderstorm. Lightning is even more likely to strike there! You and the tree are two lightning rods standing together.

Water is also a good conductor of electricity. You must never go into the water when a storm is brewing. The air becomes charged. The charge attracts lightning. The lightning has to go somewhere, and it may go into the water. That is why lifeguards order everyone out of the pool even before a storm comes.

If a thunderstorm comes up when you are boating, get to shore fast. Do not hold fishing rods or other metal objects. They attract lightning.

A car is a good, safe place to be in a thunderstorm. The rubber tires "ground" the car's metal body and remove its charge. This means the electricity cannot go through the car. Lightning does not strike cars. You are safe inside a car.

1. What should you do if you are in a field when a thunderstorm begins? _____

_____

2. What is your body like if you are outside during a thunderstorm?

_____

3. Why do lifeguards order people from the pool before a thunderstorm?

_____

4. Where is a good place to be during a thunderstorm? _____

_____

5. Besides the human body, name two things that attract lightning. _____

_____

Name: _____

Review

Directions: Review what you learned about rain, thunder and lightning. Then answer the questions.

1. How are thunderstorms different from rain showers? _____

_____

_____

2. Do you think thunderstorms are scary? Explain. _____

_____

3. What is thunder? _____

_____

4. Why do you think some thunder is louder or softer than other thunder? _____

_____

5. Why shouldn't you be outside in a storm? _____

_____

6. Name ways you can seek shelter during a storm if you are:

outside: _____

in the woods: _____

in a field: _____

in a field with no hole: _____

7. What makes a car a safe place during a storm? _____

_____

8. Would you have thought this to be true? Why or why not? _____

_____

Name: _____

Comprehension: Hurricanes

Directions: Read about hurricanes. Then answer the questions.

Have you ever been in a hurricane? If you are lucky, you have not. Hurricanes are deadly! Thunderstorms are scary and can cause damage, but hurricanes are the most destructive storms on Earth.

There are three "ingredients" in a hurricane. They are turbulent oceans, fierce winds and lashing rains. Hurricane winds can blow as fast as 180 miles (290 kilometers) an hour. They can pull up trees, buildings, cars and people. Hurricanes can destroy anything in their paths.

There are other names for hurricanes. In some parts of the world, they are called cyclones. The people who live on the islands in the Pacific Ocean call them typhoons. In Australia, some people use a funny name to describe these terrible storms. They call them "willy-willies."

Although hurricanes can occur in most parts of the world, they all start in the same place. The place hurricanes are "born" is over the ocean near the equator.

Here is how a hurricane is born. At the equator, the sun is very, very hot. The scorching sun beats down on the ocean water. It heats the water and the air above the water. The heated air begins to spiral upward in tiny, hot circles. When the heated air combines with moist air, it is drawn farther up toward the sky.

The spiral of heated air and moist air begins to twist. As it twists, it grows. As it grows, it spins faster and faster in a counterclockwise direction. (This means in the opposite direction from the way a clock's hands move.) Huge rain clouds form at the top of the spiral as the air at the top is cooled. The combination of rain, hot air and spiraling winds creates a hurricane.

1. What are other names for hurricanes? _____

_____

2. Where do all hurricanes begin? _____

_____

3. What direction does a hurricane's spiral move?

_____

4. What three "ingredients" are needed to produce a hurricane? _____

_____

Recognizing Details: Hurricanes

Directions: Review what you learned about hurricanes. Then answer the questions

1. What is the most destructive type of storm on Earth? _____

2. What makes them so destructive? _____

_____

_____

3. What makes hurricanes scarier than thunderstorms? _____

_____

4. How do hurricanes form? _____

_____

_____

5. What parts of the United States are most likely to be struck by a hurricane?

_____

_____

6. Many people enjoy living or vacationing in beach areas. Do you think they would feel the same way if they were on the coast when a hurricane happened? Explain.

_____

_____

_____

_____

7. What does counterclockwise mean? _____

_____

_____

Name: _____

Main Idea: Tornadoes

Directions: Read about tornadoes. Then answer the questions.

Another type of dangerous weather condition is a tornado. While hurricanes form over water, tornadoes form over land. Tornadoes are more likely to form in some locations than in others. The areas where tornadoes frequently form are called "tornado belts." In the United States, a major tornado belt is the basin of land between Missouri and Mississippi.

Tornadoes are formed when masses of hot air meet masses of cold air. When these air masses slam together, bad thunderstorms begin. People in tornado belts are fearful when a severe storm threatens. They know a tornado may occur if the warm, moist air rushes upward and begins to spiral.

The tornado forms a funnel cloud. The funnel is narrow at the base and broad at the top. The tornado's funnel cloud can move very fast. The winds around the funnel can move 300 miles an hour. The winds inside the funnel are fast, too. The tornado acts like a giant vacuum cleaner. It sucks up everything in its path. People, animals, cars and houses are all in danger when a tornado strikes.

It is difficult to stay out of a tornado's path. The way it moves is unpredictable. It may move straight or in a zig-zag pattern. The winds of the tornado make a screaming noise like a huge train rushing by. People who have lived through a tornado usually say it was the most frightening experience of their lives.

1. What is the main idea? (Check one.)

_____ Tornadoes form over land and hurricanes form over water.

_____ Tornados sound like a rushing train.

_____ Tornadoes, which form over land under certain weather conditions, are dangerous and frightening.

2. How fast can the winds around the funnel cloud move? _____

_____

3. Why is it hard to stay out of the path of a tornado? _____

_____

4. What household appliance can a tornado be compared to? _____

_____

Name: _____

Recognizing Details: Tornadoes

Directions: Review what you learned about tornadoes. Then answer the questions.

1. How do tornadoes form? _____

_____

2. What shape is a tornado? _____

3. What makes a tornado so dangerous? _____

_____

4. Which type of storm do you think is more dangerous, a tornado or a hurricane? Why?

_____

5. What types of weather conditions are not dangerous? _____

_____

6. What types of winter storms are also dangerous? Why? _____

_____

Directions: Compare and contrast tornadoes and hurricanes in the Venn diagram.

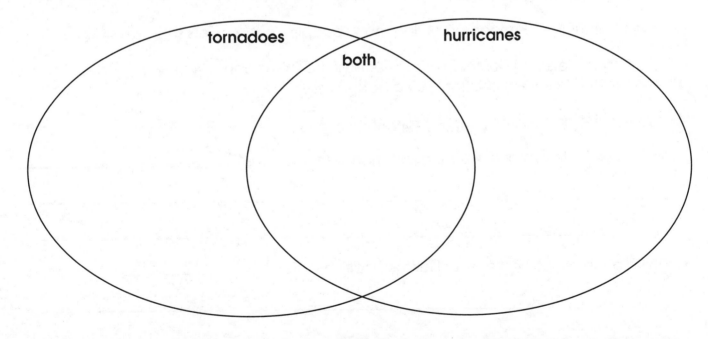

tornadoes   both   hurricanes

Review

Directions: Read this Native American legend about Lightning. Then answer the questions.

In the beginning, Lightning lived on Earth among people. Soon, he became so powerful that people were afraid. He lashed out and killed some of them. The people grew to hate him.

After Lightning had killed many people, the chiefs of the tribes got together. They had to decide what to do about Lightning. They agreed to tell Lightning he could no longer live on Earth. He begged to stay, but the chiefs forced him to leave.

Shortly after Lightning left, a great monster began to carry people away. The monster lived deep underground. The people could not kill the monster. He always escaped underground before they could catch him.

Lightning heard about their trouble. He came back to the chiefs. "I will kill the monster," he told them. "But in return, you must let me live among you again."

Because he was the only one who could kill the great monster, the chiefs let Lightning return. He did not change his ways much. He is still dangerous. To this day, that is why we have Lightning on Earth.

1. What is the main idea? (Check one.)

   _____ Lightning was mean and killed many people, so the chiefs sent him away.

   _____ The chiefs sent Lightning away because he was mean, but they agreed to let him return to save them from the great monster.

   _____ There are worse things than Lightning.

2. Why couldn't the people kill the great monster themselves? _____

   _____

   _____

3. Why did the chiefs agree to let Lightning return to Earth? _____

   _____

Review

Directions: Write your own Native American legend about Tornado or Hurricane.

_____

_____

_____

_____

_____

_____

_____

_____

_____

_____

_____

_____

_____

_____

_____

_____

_____

_____

_____

Glossary

Comprehension: Understanding what is seen, heard or read.

Main Idea: The most important point of a story or article.

Following Directions: Doing what the directions say to do.

Recognizing Details: Being able to pick out and remember the who, what, when, where, why and how of what is read.

Sequencing: Putting things or events in order.

Answer Key

Comprehension: "The Princess and the Pea"

Fairy tales are short stories written for children involving magical characters.

Directions: Read the story. Then answer the questions.

Once there was a prince who wanted to get married. The catch was, he had to marry a *real* princess. The Prince knew that real princesses were few and far between. When they heard he was looking for a bride, many young women came to the palace. All claimed to be real princesses.

"Hmmm," thought the Prince. "I must think of a way to sort out the real princesses from the fake ones. I will ask the Queen for advice."

Luckily, since he was a prince, the Queen was also his mother. So of course she had her son's best interests at heart. "A real princess is very delicate," said the Queen. "She must sleep on a mattress as soft as a cloud. If there is even a small lump, she will not be able to sleep."

"Why not?" asked the Prince. He was a nice man but not as smart as his mother.

"Because she is so delicate!" said the Queen impatiently. "Let's figure out a way to test her. Better still, let me figure out a test. You go down and pick a girl to try out my plan."

The Prince went down to the lobby of the castle. A very pretty but humble-looking girl caught his eye. He brought her back to his mother, who welcomed her.

"Please be our guest at the castle tonight," said the Queen. "Tomorrow we will talk with you about whether you are a real princess."

The pretty but humble girl was shown to her room. In it was a pile of five mattresses, all fluffy and clean. "A princess is delicate," said the Queen. "Sweet dreams!"

The girl climbed to the top of the pile and laid down, but she could not sleep. She tossed and turned and was quite cross the next morning.

"I found this under the fourth mattress when I got up this morning," she said. She handed a small green pea to the Queen. "No wonder I couldn't sleep!"

The Queen clapped her hands. The Prince looked confused. "A real princess is delicate. If this pea I put under the mattress kept you awake, you are definitely a princess."

"Of course I am," said the Princess. "Now may I please take a nap?"

1. Why does the Prince worry about finding a bride? **His bride must be a real princess and real princesses are hard to find.**

2. According to the Queen, how can the Prince tell who is a real princess? **A real princess is very delicate.**

3. Who hides something under the girl's mattress? **the Queen**

3

Comprehension: "The Princess and the Pea"

Directions: Review the story "The Princess and the Pea." Then answer the questions.

1. Why does the Prince need a test to see who is a real princess? **Many young women wanted to marry him, but the Prince could only marry a "real" princess.**

2. Why does the Princess have trouble sleeping? **There was a pea under her mattress.**

3. In this story, the Queen puts a small pea under a pile of mattresses to see if the girl is delicate. What else could be done to test a princess for delicacy? _Answers will vary._

The story does not tell whether or not the Prince and the Princess got married and live happily ever after, only that the Princess wanted a nap.

Directions: Write a new ending to the story.

4. What do you think happens after the Princess takes a nap? _Answers will vary._

4

Comprehension: "The Frog Prince"

Directions: Read the story "The Frog Prince." Then answer the questions.

Once upon a time, there lived a beautiful princess who liked to play alone in the woods. One day, as she was playing with her golden ball, it rolled into a lake. The water was so deep she could not see the ball. The Princess was very sad. She cried out, "I would give anything to have my golden ball back!"

Suddenly, a large ugly frog popped out of the water. "Anything?" he croaked. The Princess looked at him with distaste. "Yes," she said. "I would give anything."

"I will get your golden ball," said the frog. "In return, you must take me back to the castle. You must let me live with you and eat from your golden plate."

"Whatever you want," said the Princess. She thought the frog was very ugly, but she wanted her golden ball.

The frog dove down and brought the ball to the Princess. She put the frog in her pocket and took him home. "He is ugly," the Princess said. "But a promise is a promise. And a princess always keeps her word."

The Princess changed her clothes and forgot all about the frog. That evening, she heard a tapping at her door. She ran to the door to open it and a handsome prince stepped in.

"Who are you?" asked the Princess, already half in love.

"I am the prince you rescued at the lake," said the handsome Prince. "I was turned into a frog one hundred years ago today by a wicked lady. Because they always keep their promises, only a beautiful princess could break the spell. You are a little forgetful, but you did keep your word!"

Can you guess what happened next? Of course, they were married and lived happily ever after.

1. What does the frog ask the Princess to promise? **to take him back to the castle, let him live with her and eat from her golden plate.**

2. Where does the Princess put the frog when she leaves the lake? **in her pocket**

3. Why could only a princess break the spell? **Because they always keep their promises.**

5

Comprehension: "The Frog Prince"

Directions: Review the story "The Frog Prince." Then answer the questions.

1. What does the Princess lose in the lake? **a golden ball**

2. How does she get it back? **A frog dove to the bottom of the lake and got it for her in return for a promise from the Princess.**

3. How does the frog turn back into a prince? **The spell is broken when the Princess keeps her word.**

4. What phrases are used to begin and end this story? **"once upon a time" and "happily ever after"**

5. Are these words used frequently to begin and end fairy tales? **yes**

There is more than one version of most fairy tales. In another version of this story, the Princess has to kiss the frog in order for him to change back into a prince.

Directions: Write your answers.

6. What do you think would happen in a story ~~where the~~ Princess kisses the frog, but he remains a ~~frog~~?

7. What kinds of problems ~~would she have~~ with a bossy frog in the castle? Brainstorm ideas and write them ~~down~~.

8. Rewrite the ~~story of "The~~ Frog Prince" so that the frog remains a frog and does not turn into a handso~~me prince~~.

Answers will vary.

6

Creative Writing: Your Own Fairy Tale

All stories need a **beginning**, a **middle** and an **ending**. The beginning introduces the characters and the setting. It tells what problem needs to be solved.

The middle of a story shows the action—what the characters try to do to solve the problem.

The ending of a story tells how the characters solved the problem and what happened at the end.

Directions: Write your own fairy tale.

Beginning

Middle

Ending

Answers will vary.

7

Review

Directions: Think of fairy tales you know from books or videos, like "Cinderella," "Snow White," "Sleeping Beauty," "Rapunzel" and "Beauty and the Beast." Then answer the questions.

1. What are some common elements in all fairy tales? **Answers may include: a hero or heroine, a villain, a problem, a happy ending**

2. How do fairy tales usually begin? **"Once upon a time"**

3. How do fairy tales usually end? **with a happy ending**

Directions: Locate and read several different versions of the same fairy tale. For example: "Cinderella," "Princess Furball," "Cinderlad" and "Yah Shen." Then answer the questions.

4. How are the stories alike?

5. How are they different?

6. Which ~~version did you like best?~~ ~~the author?~~

7. Which sh~~ould?~~ ~~est? Why?~~

Answers will vary.

8

Review

Most of us have read many fairy tales and have seen them in movies. Fairy tales have a certain style and format they usually follow.

Directions: Use another sheet of paper to write another fairy tale. Use the following questions to help you brainstorm ideas.

1. What is the name of the kingdom?

2. What is the size of the kingdom, its climate, trees, plants, animals, etc.?

3. What kind of magic happens there?

4. Who are the characters?
   Good guys   Bad guys

5. What does each char—

6. What kind of—   —icular character and why?

Answers will vary.

7. What happens to the good characters and the bad characters in the end?

9

Following Directions: Early Native Americans

Directions: Read about the early Native Americans. Then work the puzzle.

There were about 300 Native American tribes in North America when the first white settlers came to New England in the 1500s. These Native Americans loved and respected the earth. They hunted buffalo on the plains. They fished in the clear rivers. They planted corn and beans on the rich land. They gathered roots and herbs. Before the white settlers drove them out, the Native Americans were masters of the land and all its riches.

The Native Americans grew crops, hunted for food, made clothing and built their homes from what they found on the land in the area where they lived. That is why each tribe of Native Americans was different. Some Native Americans lived in special tents called tepees. Some lived in adobe pueblos. Some lived in simple huts called hogans.

Crossword puzzle:
- P U E B L O S
- B U F F A L O
- T E P E E S
- T H R E E (down)
- H O G A N (down)
- H E A R T H (down)

Across:
2. Native American homes made of adobe
3. Native Americans hunted this animal.
4. Tents some Native Americans lived in

Down:
1. Huts some Native Americans lived in
4. There were this many hundred tribes of Native Americans when settlers came.
5. All the tribes loved the _____

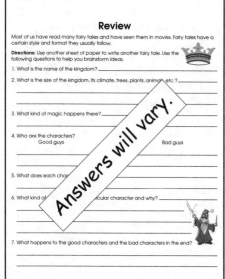

10

Comprehension: The Pueblo People

Directions: Read about the Pueblo people. Then answer the questions.

Long ago, Native Americans occupied all the land that is now Arizona, New Mexico, Utah and parts of California and Colorado. Twenty-five different tribes lived in this southwestern area. Several of the tribes lived in villages called pueblos. The Hopi (hope-ee) Indians lived in pueblos. So did the Zuñi (zoo-nee) and the Laguna (lah-goon-nah). These and other tribes who lived in villages were called the "Pueblo people."

When it was time for the Pueblo people to plant crops, everyone helped. The men kept the weeds pulled. Native Americans prayed for rain to make their crops grow. As part of their worship, they also had special dances called rain dances. When it was time for harvest, the women helped.

The land was bountiful to the Pueblo people. They grew many different crops. They planted beans, squash and 19 different kinds of corn. They gathered wild nuts and berries. They hunted for deer and rabbits. They also traded with other tribes for things they could not grow or hunt.

The Pueblo people lived in unusual houses. Their homes were made of adobe brick. Adobe is a type of mud. They shaped the mud into bricks, dried them, then built with them. Many adobe homes exist today in the Southwest.

The adobe homes of long ago had no doors. The Pueblo people entered through a type of trapdoor at the top. The homes were three or four stories high. The ground floor had no windows and was used for storage. These adobe homes were clustered around a central plaza. Each village had several clusters of homes. Villages also had two or three clubhouses where people could gather for celebrations. Each village also had places for worship.

1. What were the five states where the Pueblo people lived? _Arizona, Utah New Mexico, California, Colorado_

2. What were three crops the Pueblo people grew? _beans, squash, corn_

3. The early pueblo houses had no
☐ yards.   ☐ windows.   ☑ doors.

11

Recognizing Details: The Pueblo People

"At the edge of the world
It grows light.
The trees stand shining."
(Pueblo poem)

Directions: Read more about the Pueblo people. Then answer the questions.

The Pueblo people were peaceful. They loved nature, and they seldom fought in wars. When they did fight, it was to protect their people or their land. Their dances, too, were gentle. The Pueblo people danced to ask the gods to bring rain or sunshine. Sometimes they asked the gods to help the women have children.

Some Native Americans wore masks when they danced. The masks were called kachinas (ka-chee-nas). They represented the faces of dead ancestors. (Ancestors are all the family members who have lived and died before.)

The Pueblo people were talented at crafts. The men of many tribes made beautiful jewelry. The women made pottery and painted it with beautiful colors. They traded some of the things they made with people from other tribes.

Both boys and girls needed their parents' permission to marry. After they married, they were given a room next to the bride's mother. If the marriage did not work out, sometimes the groom moved back home again.

1. Among the Pueblo people, who made jewelry? _the men_

2. Who made pottery? _the women_

3. What did some of the Pueblo people wear when they danced? _masks called kachinas_

4. Why did the Pueblo people dance for the gods? _to ask the gods for rain or sunshine or help with childbirth_

5. Where did newly married couples live? _in a room next to the bride's mother_

6. Why would a man move back home after marriage? _He would move out if the marriage did not work out._

12

Recognizing Details: The Pueblo People

Directions: Review what you learned about the Pueblo people. Then answer the questions.

1. How many different tribes lived in the Southwestern part of the United States? _25_

2. The article specifically names three of the Pueblo tribes. Where could you find the names of the other Pueblo tribes? _reference sources like encyclopedias or the Internet_

3. How did the Pueblo people build their adobe homes? _They shaped mud into bricks, dried them, then built with them._

4. How did the location and climate affect their lifestyle? _Location and climate affected what they wore, what crops they grew, the animals they hunted and materials used for building homes._

5. How were the jobs of the men and women of a Pueblo tribe alike? _Both helped care for crops._

6. How were their jobs different? _Men made jewelry. Women made pottery._

7. How do the responsibilities of the Pueblo men and women discussed differ from those of men and women today? _Answers will vary._

13

Comprehension: A California Tribe

Directions: Read about the Yuma. Then answer the questions.

California was home to many Native Americans. The weather was warm, and food was plentiful. California was an ideal place to live.

One California tribe that made good use of the land was the Yuma. The Yuma farmed and gathered roots and berries. They harvested dozens of wild plants. They ground them up and used them in cooking. The Yuma mixed acorns with flour and water to make a kind of oatmeal. They fished in California's rich waters. They hunted deer and small game. The Yuma made the most of what Mother Nature offered.

The Yuma lived in huts. The roofs were made of dirt. The walls were made of grass. Some Yuma lived together in huts - big round buildings made with poles and woven grasses. As many as 50 people lived in these large homes.

Like other tribes, the Yuma made crafts. Their woven baskets were especially beautiful. The women also wove cradles, hats, bowls and other useful items for the tribe.

When it was time to marry, a boy's parents chose a 15-year-old girl for him. The girl was a Yuma, too, but from another village. Except for the chief, each man took only one wife.

When a Yuma died, a big ceremony was held. The Yumas had great respect for death. After someone died, his or her name was never spoken again.

1. What were two reasons why California was an ideal place to live? _The weather was warm and food was plentiful._

2. What did the Yuma use acorns for? _They ground them up and used them for cooking._

3. What was a beautiful craft made by the Yuma? _woven baskets_

4. How old was a Yuma bride? _15_

5. What types of homes did the Yuma live in? _dirt and grass huts_

6. How did the Yuma feel about death? _They had great respect for death._

14

Recognizing Details: The Yuma

Directions: Review what you read about the Yuma. Write the answers.

1. How did the Yuma make good use of the land?
   They farmed and gathered roots, acorns and berries.
   They fished and hunted.

2. How were the Yuma like the Pueblo people? Both hunted deer and
   small game, farmed, gathered berries and made crafts.

3. How were they different? The Yuma fished, made baskets and
   lived in huts. The Pueblos made pottery and jewelry and
   lived in adobe homes.

4. Why did the Yuma have homes different than those of the Pueblo tribes?
   Answers should indicate differences in natural materials
   available due to different climates.

5. When it was time for a young Yuma man to marry, his parents selected a fifteen-year-old bride for him from another tribe. Do you think this is a good idea? Why or why not?

   Answers will vary.

6. Why do you suppose the Yuma _____ person's name after he/she died?

7. Do you think this _____ thing to do? Explain your answer. _____

15

Following Directions: Sailor Native Americans

Directions: Read about the Sailor Native Americans of Puget Sound. Then work the puzzle.

Three tribes lived on Puget (pew-jit) Sound in Washington state. They made their living from the sea. People later called them the "Sailor" Indians.

These Native Americans fished for salmon. They trapped the salmon in large baskets. Sometimes they used large nets. The sea was filled with fish. Their nets rarely came up empty. The Sailor Native Americans also gathered roots and berries. They hunted deer, black bear and ducks.

Their homes were amazing! They built big wooden buildings without nails. They did not use saws to cut the wood. The walls and roofs were tied together. Each building had different homes inside. As many as 50 families lived in each big building.

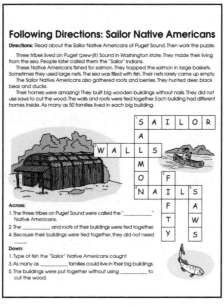

Crossword:
Across 1: SAILOR, Down/across forming: SALMON, WALLS, NAILS with FIFTY, SAWS

Across:
1. The three tribes on Puget Sound were called the "_____" Native Americans.
2. The _____ and roofs of their buildings were tied together.
4. Because their buildings were tied together, they did not need _____.

Down:
1. Type of fish the "Sailor" Native Americans caught
3. As many as _____ families could live in their big buildings.
5. The buildings were put together without using _____ to cut the wood.

16

Following Directions: Sailor Native Americans

Directions: Review what you read about the Sailor Native Americans. Write your answers.

1. How were the housing arrangements of the Puget Sound Native Americans similar to those of the Yuma?
   Many families lived together in large buildings.

2. How was the diet of the Sailor Native Americans like those of the Yuma and Pueblo?
   All three hunted and gathered berries.

3. How was it different? Yumas and Pueblos grew their own crops.

4. The Sailor Native Americans made a living from the sea, and their nets were rarely empty. What type of transportation do you think these Native Americans used to get their nets to the sea?
   canoes, boats or rafts

5. Where could you find more information on this group of Native Americans to check your answer?
   reference sources like encyclopedias and the Internet

6. Verify your answer. Were you correct? Answers will vary.

7. Who do you think performed the many tasks in the Sailor village? Write men, women, boys and/or girls for your answers.

   Built homes? _____
   Fished? _____ and berries?
   Hunted game? _____ Made fishing nets? ____
   Answers will vary.

8. The homes of the Sailor Native Americans could be compared to what type of modern dwelling?
   apartment buildings or condos

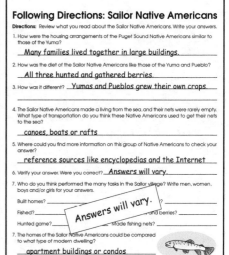

17

Recognizing Details: The Woodlands People

Directions: Read about the Woodlands People. Then answer the questions.

The Southeast Woodlands people lived in a huge wooded area. The 15 tribes that lived in the Southeast Woodlands were very different from the Pueblo people of the Southwest.

The Woodlands people liked war. Boys could not wait to grow up and become warriors! It was a mark of manhood to fight. They carried clubs and shields. They used bows, arrows and long spears. Many of the Woodlands people took the scalps of their victims.

Many warriors had tattoos. Tattoos are pictures on the skin. Tattoos were marks of bravery in battle. A man with many tattoos was a hero.

These Southeast Woodlands people lived in different types of homes. Because it was hot, the houses of some tribes in what is now Florida did not have walls. The Seminole (sem-in-ole) houses had floors raised off the ground. The roofs were made of reeds, which are a type of grass.

In warm weather, the Woodlands people often went barefoot. In cold weather, they wore moccasins (mock-ah-sins) on their feet. Men wore buckskin pants and women wore buckskin skirts. Their clothes were made from the hides of deer. When it was very cold, they wore beaver robes to keep warm.

1. What are two ways the Woodlands people were different from the Pueblos?
   Answers will vary.

2. What are four things the Woodlands people used in battle?
   clubs, shields, bows, arrows, spears

Directions: Check the correct answer.

3. In warm weather, Woodland Native Americans
   ☐ wore moccasins. ☑ went barefoot. ☐ wore cowboy boots.

4. When it was cold, they wrapped themselves in
   ☑ beaver robes. ☐ cotton shawls. ☐ buffalo robes.

18

Sequencing: Kanati's Son

A **legend** is a story or group of stories handed down through generations. Legends are usually about an actual person.

Directions: Read about Kanati's son. Then number the events in order.

This legend is told by a tribe called the Cherokee (chair-oh-key).

Long ago, soon after the world was made, a hunter and his wife lived on a big mountain with their son. The father's name was Kanati (kah-na-tee), which means "lucky hunter." The mother's name was Selu (see-loo), which means "corn." No one remembers the son's name.

The little boy used to play alone by the river each day. One day, elders of the tribe told the boy's parents they had heard two children playing. Since their boy was the only child around, the parents were puzzled. They told their son what the elders had said.

"I do have a playmate," the boy said. "He comes out of the river. He says he is the brother that mother threw in the river."

Then Selu knew what had happened.

"He is formed from the blood of the animals I washed in the river," she told Kanati. "After you kill them, I wash them in the river before I cook them."

Here is what Kanati told his boy: "Tomorrow when the other boy comes, wrestle with him. Hold him to the ground and call for us."

The boy did as his parents told him. When he called, they came running and grabbed the wild boy. They took him home and tried to tame him. The boy grew up with magic powers. The Cherokee called this "adawehi" (ad-da-we-hi). He was always getting into mischief! But he saved himself with his magic.

_5_ Selu and Kanati try to tame the boy from the river.

_3_ The little boy tells Selu and Kanati about the other boy.

_2_ The little boy's parents are puzzled.

_6_ The new boy grows up with magic powers.

_1_ The elders tell Selu and Kanati they heard two children playing.

_4_ The little boy wrestles his new playmate to the ground.

19

Comprehension: "Why Owls Have Big Eyes"

Directions: Read the Native American legend "Why Owls Have Big Eyes." Then answer the questions.

Creator made all the animals, one by one. He made each one the way they wanted to look. Owl interrupted when Creator was making Rabbit.

"Whooo, whooo," he said. "Make me now. I want a long neck like Swan, red feathers like Cardinal and a sharp beak like Eagle. Make me the most beautiful bird in the world."

"Quiet!" shouted Creator. "I am making Rabbit. Turn around and wait your turn."

Creator made Rabbit's long ears and long back legs. Before he could make Rabbit's long front legs, Owl interrupted again.

"Whooo, whooo," Owl said. "Make me now. Make me the most beautiful bird in the world."

"Close your eyes. No one may watch me work," said Creator. "Wait your turn. Do not interrupt again."

Owl would not wait. He was very rude. "I will watch if I want to," he said.

"All right then," said Creator. "I will make you now."

He pushed Owl's head until it was close to his body. He shook Owl until his eyes grew big with fright. He pulled on Owl's ears so they stuck out on both sides. Then he covered Owl's feathers with mud.

"There," he said. "That's what you get for not waiting your turn. You have big ears to listen so you can hear when you are told what to do. You have big eyes, but you can't watch me with them. I work only in the day and you will be awake only at night. Your feathers will forever be the color of mud, not red like Cardinal's."

When he heard Creator's words, Owl flew away. Creator turned to finish Rabbit, but Rabbit had run away before Creator could finish his front legs or give him sharp claws to defend himself. To this day, rabbits have short front legs, are afraid of owls and, cannot defend themselves. And that's why owls have short necks, big eyes, brownish feathers and ears that stick out.

1. According to this legend, who made all the animals? Creator

2. Why did Rabbit run away before Creator finished making him?
   He was afraid.

3. Why didn't Creator make Owl beautiful? because Owl would not wait
   his turn

4. Why are rabbits afraid of owls? Owls hunt rabbits.

20

Review

Review what you read about Native Americans. Then answer the questions.

1. Of the tribes discussed, which one would you most like to have been a member of? Explain your answer.

   <u>Answers will vary.</u>

2. Why did each of the tribes have a different lifestyle? <u>because of their location, different climates and resources were available.</u>

3. How did their location influence how each of the tribes functioned? <u>Food, plants, animals, fish, climate and building materials all influenced the people and how they lived.</u>

Directions: Select two of the Native American tribes you read about. Compare and contrast their homes, clothing and lifestyle in the Venn diagram. Write words and phrases that were unique to one group or the other in the correct parts of the circle. Write words and phrases that are common to both groups in the section where the circles intersect.

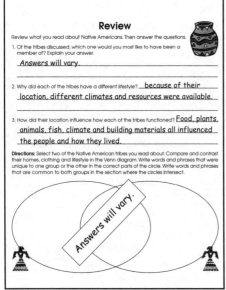

Answers will vary.

21

Review

Directions: Review what you learned about Native Americans. Write your answers on the lines.

1. Select one of the Native American tribes and write about how their lives would be different today.

2. Do research using an encyclopedia, books on _____ the Internet. Find out how some of these tribes are living toda_____ aph about what you learned.

3. Use reference _____ ut Native Americans that once lived in your area. Write a pa_____ their lifestyle.

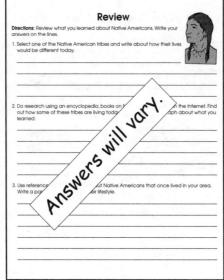

Answers will vary.

22

Main Idea: "The Hare and the Tortoise"

The story of "The Hare and the Tortoise" is called a **fable**. Fables are usually short stories. As you read this story and the other fables on the next few pages, look for two characteristics the fables have in common.

Directions: Read the fable "The Hare and the Tortoise." Then answer the questions.

One day the hare and the tortoise were talking. Or rather, the hare was bragging and the tortoise was listening.

"I am faster than the wind," bragged the hare. "I feel sorry for you because you are so slow! Why, you are the slowest fellow I have ever seen."

"Do you think so?" asked the tortoise with a smile. "I will race you to that big tree across the field."

Slowly, he lifted a leg. Slowly, he pointed toward the tree.

"Ha!" scoffed the hare. "You must be kidding! You will most certainly be the loser! But, if you insist, we will race."

The tortoise nodded politely. "I'll be off," he said. Slowly and steadily, the tortoise moved across the field.

The hare stood back and laughed. "How sad that he should compete with me!" he said. His chest puffed up with pride. "I will take a little nap while the poor old tortoise lumbers along. When I wake up, he will still be only halfway across the field."

The tortoise kept on, slow and steady, across the field. Some time later, the hare awoke. He discovered that while he slept, the tortoise had won the race.

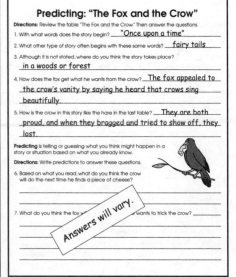

1. What is the main idea? (Check one.)

   _____ Tortoises are faster than hares.

   _____ Hares need more sleep than tortoises.

   __✓__ Slow and steady wins the race.

2. The hare brags that he is faster than what? (Check one.)

   _____ a bullet

   _____ a greyhound

   __✓__ the wind

3. Who is modest, the tortoise or the hare? <u>the tortoise</u>

23

Cause and Effect: "The Hare and the Tortoise"

Another important skill in reading is recognizing cause and effect. The **cause** is the reason something happens. The **effect** is what happens or the situation that results from the cause. In the story, the hare falling asleep is a cause. It causes the hare to lose the race. Losing the race is the effect.

Directions: Identify the underlined words or phrases by writing **cause** or **effect** on the blanks.

1. <u>The hare and tortoise had a race</u> because the hare bragged about being faster.   _effect_

2. <u>The tortoise won the race</u> because he continued on, slowly, but steadily.   _cause_

Directions: Review the fable "The Hare and the Tortoise." Then answer the questions.

1. Who are the two main characters? <u>hare and tortoise</u>

2. Where does the story take place? <u>in a field with trees</u>

3. What lessons can be learned from this story? <u>slow and steady wins the race, people shouldn't brag</u>

4. The lesson that is learned at the end of a fable has a special name. What is that special name? <u>moral</u>

5. Why did the hare want to race the tortoise? <u>to prove he was faster</u>

6. How do you think the hare felt at the end of the story?

7. How do you think the tortoise felt at the e___

Answers will vary.

24

Sequencing: "The Fox and the Crow"

Directions: Read the fable "The Fox and the Crow." Then number the events in order.

Once upon a time, a crow found a piece of cheese on the ground. "Aha!" he said to himself. "This dropped from a workman's sandwich. It will make a fine lunch for me."

The crow picked up the cheese in his beak. He flew to a tree to eat it. Just as he began to chew it, a fox trotted by.

"Hello, crow!" he said slyly, for he wanted the cheese. The fox knew if the crow answered, the cheese would fall from its mouth. Then the fox would have cheese for lunch!

The crow just nodded.

"It's a wonderful day, isn't it?" asked the fox.

The crow nodded again and held onto the cheese.

"You are the most beautiful bird I have ever seen," added the fox.

The crow spread his feathers. Everyone likes a compliment. Still, the crow held firmly to the cheese.

"There is something I have heard," said the fox, "and I wonder if it is true. I heard that you sing more sweetly than any of the other birds."

The crow was eager to show off his talents. He opened his beak to sing. The cheese dropped to the ground.

"I said you were beautiful," said the fox as he ran away with the cheese. "I did not say you were smart!"

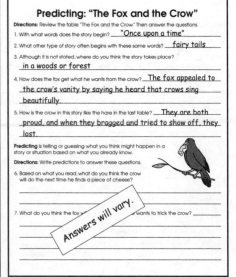

   _7_ The crow drops the cheese.

   _3_ The crow flies to a tree with the cheese.

   _5_ The fox tells the crow he is beautiful.

   _8_ The fox runs off with the cheese.

   _1_ A workman loses the cheese from his sandwich.

   _4_ The fox comes along.

   _6_ The fox tells the crow he has heard that crows sing beautifully.

   _2_ The crow picks up the cheese.

25

Predicting: "The Fox and the Crow"

Directions: Review the fable "The Fox and the Crow." Then answer the questions.

1. With what words does the story begin? <u>"Once upon a time"</u>

2. What other type of story often begins with these same words? <u>fairy tails</u>

3. Although it is not stated, where do you think the story takes place? <u>in a woods or forest</u>

4. How does the fox get what he wants from the crow? <u>The fox appealed to the crow's vanity by saying he heard that crows sing beautifully.</u>

5. How is the crow in this story like the hare in the last fable? <u>They are both proud, and when they bragged and tried to show off, they lost.</u>

Predicting is telling or guessing what you think might happen in a story or situation based on what you already know.

Directions: Write predictions to answer these questions.

6. Based on what you read, what do you think the crow will do the next time he finds a piece of cheese?

7. What do you think the fox w_____ wants to trick the crow?

Answers will vary.

26

Following Directions: "The Boy Who Cried Wolf"

Directions: Read the fable "The Boy Who Cried Wolf." Then complete the puzzle.

Once there was a shepherd boy who tended his sheep alone. Sheep are gentle animals. They are easy to take care of. The boy grew bored.

"I can't stand another minute alone with these sheep," he said crossly. He knew only one thing would bring people quickly to him. If he cried, "Wolf!" the men in the village would run up the mountain. They would come to help save the sheep from the wolf.

"Wolf!" he yelled loudly, and he blew on his horn.

Quick as a wink, a dozen men came running. When they realized it was a joke, they were very angry. The boy promised never to do it again. But a week later, he grew bored and cried, "Wolf!" again. Again, the men ran to him. This time they were very, very angry.

Soon afterwards, a wolf really came. The boy was scared. "Wolf!" he cried. "Wolf! Wolf! Wolf!"

He blew his horn, but no one came, and the wolf ate all his sheep.

Crossword puzzle: M O U N T A I N (with V I L L A G E, S C A R E D, G E N T L E, M E N)

Across:
2. This is where the boy tends sheep.
4. When no one came, the wolf ___ all the sheep.
5. Sheep are ___ and easy to take care of.

Down:
1. The people who come are from here.
2. At first, when the boy cries, "Wolf!" the ___ come running.
3. When a wolf really comes, this is how the boy feels.

27

Cause and Effect: "The Boy Who Cried Wolf"

Directions: Identify the underlined words as a cause or an effect.

1. The boy cries wolf because he is bored. _____ effect
2. The boy blows his horn and the men come running. _____ effect
3. No one comes, and the wolf eats all the sheep. _____ effect

Directions: Answer the questions.

4. What lesson can be learned from this story? _Sample answer:_
always tell the truth.

5. How is this story like the two other fables you read?

6. Is the boy in the story more like the fox o[...]

Answers will vary.

28

Comprehension: "The City Mouse and the Country Mouse"

Directions: Read the fable "The City Mouse and the Country Mouse." Then answer the questions.

Once there were two mice, a city mouse and a country mouse. They were cousins. The country mouse was always begging his cousin to visit him. Finally, the city mouse agreed.

When he arrived, the city mouse was not very polite. "How do you stand it here?" he asked, wrinkling his nose. "All you have to eat is corn and barley. All you have to wear is old, tattered work clothes. And all you have to listen to are the other animals. Why don't you come and visit me? Then you will see what it's like to really live!"

The country mouse liked corn and barley. He liked the sounds of the other animals. And he liked his old work clothes fine. Secretly, he thought his cousin was silly to wear fancy clothes. Still, the city sounded exciting. Why not give it a try?

Since he had no clothes to pack, the country mouse was ready in no time. His cousin told him stories about the city as they traveled. The buildings were so high! The food was so good! The girl mice were so beautiful!

The home of the city mouse was nice. He lived in a hole in the wall in an old castle. "It is only a hole in the wall," said the city mouse, "but it is a very nice wall, indeed!"

That night, the mice crept out of the wall. Everyone had eaten, but the maid had not cleaned up. The table was still loaded with good food. The mice ate and ate. The country mouse was not used to rich food. He began to feel sick to his stomach.

Just then, they heard loud barking. Two huge dogs ran into the room. They nearly bit off the country mouse's tail! He barely made it to the hole in the wall in time. That did it!

"Thank you for showing me the city," said the country mouse, "but it is too exciting for me. I am going home where it is peaceful. I can't wait to settle my stomach with some corn and barley."

1. What are three things the city mouse says are wrong with the country? _____
no good food, old clothes to wear, animal noises

2. Why doesn't it take the country mouse long to get ready to leave with the city mouse?
He has no clothes to pack.

3. Why does the country mouse secretly think his cousin is silly? _his fancy clothes_

29

Sequencing: "The City Mouse and the Country Mouse"

Directions: Review the fable "The City Mouse and the Country Mouse." Use the Venn diagram to compare and contrast the lifestyles of the city mouse and the country mouse.

City Mouse — Both — Country Mouse

Answers will vary.

Directions: Write five [...] story, in order.

Directions: Answer these questions about the fable.

1. How do the two mice feel about each other? _They do not understand
each other's way of life._

2. Which mouse do you think is most like the hare? Why? _Answers will vary._

30

Sequencing: "The Man and the Snake"

Directions: Read the fable "The Man and the Snake." Then number the events in order.

Once, a kind man saw a snake in the road. It was winter and the poor snake was nearly frozen. The man began to walk away, but he could not.

"The snake is one of Earth's creatures, too," he said. He picked up the snake and put it in a sack. "I will take it home to warm up by my fire. Then I will set it free."

The man stopped for lunch at a village inn. He put his coat and his sack on a bench by the fireplace. He planned to sit nearby, but the inn was crowded, so he had to sit across the room.

He soon forgot about the snake. As he was eating his soup, he heard screams. Warmed by the fire, the snake had crawled from the bag. It hissed at the people near the fire.

The man jumped up and ran to the fireplace. "Is this how you repay the kindness of others?" he shouted.

He grabbed a stick used for stirring the fire and chased the snake out of the inn.

_4_ The man puts his bag down by the fireplace.
_9_ The man chases the snake.
_2_ A kind man rescues the snake.
_6_ The snake warms up and crawls out of the bag.
_3_ The man plans to take the snake home.
_5_ The man eats a bowl of soup.
_7_ The snake hisses at people.
_1_ A snake is nearly frozen in the road.
_8_ The man grabs a stick from the fireplace.

31

Sequencing: "The Wind and the Sun"

Directions: Read the fable "The Wind and the Sun." Then number the events in order.

One day, North Wind and Sun began to argue about who was stronger.

"I am stronger," declared North Wind.

"No," said Sun. "I am much stronger than you."

They argued for three days and three nights.

Finally, Sun said, "I know how we can settle the argument. See that traveler walking down the road? Whoever can make him take off his cloak first is the stronger. Do you agree?"

North Wind agreed. He wanted to try first. He blew and blew. The traveler shivered and pulled his cloak tightly around his body. North Wind sent a blast of wind so strong it almost pulled the cloak off the traveler, but the traveler only held tighter to his cloak.

Then it was Sun's turn. When Sun sent gentle, warm sunbeams, the traveler loosened his cloak. Then Sun sent his warmest beams to the traveler. After a short time, the traveler became so warm he threw off his cloak and ran to the shade of the nearest tree.

_4_ Sun sent warm beams to the traveler.
_1_ Sun and North Wind argued.
_5_ The traveler threw off his cloak and ran to the shade.
_3_ The traveler pulled his cloak tightly around his body.
_2_ North Wind blew cold air on the traveler.

Directions: Answer the questions. (Check one.)

What is the moral of this fable?
_____ Sun is stronger than North Wind.
_____ North Wind is cold.
_✓_ A kind and gentle manner works better than force.
_____ Travelers should hold on to their cloaks when the wind blows.
_____ Stay out of arguments between Sun and North Wind.

Who do you think is stronger, North Wind or Sun? Why? _Answers will vary._

32

Review

At the beginning of the section on fables, you were asked to discover two elements common to the fables.

Directions: Review the fables you read. Then answer the questions.

1. What are the two elements common to fables? **Main characters are often animals that talk and act like people. Stories teach a lesson.**

2. Each fable has a "moral" or lesson to be learned. What is the moral of each of the fables?

"The Hare and the Tortoise" _____

"The Fox and the Crow" _____

"The Boy Who Cried Wolf" _____   *Answers will vary.*

"The City Mouse and the Country Mouse" _____

"The Man and the Snake" _____

3. How do the titles of the fables give clues to what or who the fables were about? **The titles name the main characters.**

4. For each fable, write the character you think is the good character and the one you think is the bad character.

	"Good character"	"Bad character"
"The Hare and the Tortoise"		
"The Fox and the Crow"		
"The Wind and the Sun"		
"The City Mouse and the Country Mouse"		
"The Man and the Snake"		

Answers will vary.

33

Fable Writing Organizer

Fables are short stories with animals as the main characters. Each story teaches a lesson.

Directions: Select one of the following pairs of animals as characters to use for a fable of your own.

A pig and an ox	An ant and a frog	A cat and a monkey
A fly and a butterfly	A spider and a bear	A goose and a deer
A snail and a lion	A horse and a dog	A T-Rex and a shark

Directions: Fill in the outline below with words and phrases to organize a fable of your own.

Animal pair _____

Type of conflict between the animals _____

How the conflict is settled _____

Moral of the story _____

Directions: Write _____ fable a title. Illustrate it if you like.

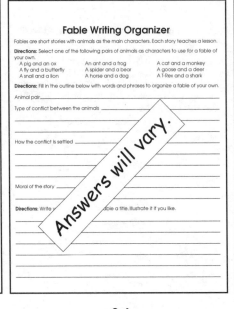

Answers will vary.

34

Recognizing Details: "Why Bear Has a Short Tail"

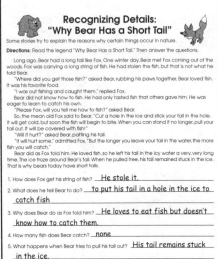

Some stories try to explain the reasons why certain things occur in nature.

Directions: Read the legend "Why Bear Has a Short Tail." Then answer the questions.

Long ago, Bear had a long tail like Fox. One winter day, Bear met Fox coming out of the woods. Fox was carrying a long string of fish. He had stolen the fish, but that is not what he told Bear.

"Where did you get those fish?" asked Bear, rubbing his paws together. Bear loved fish. It was his favorite food.

"I was out fishing and caught them," replied Fox.

Bear did not know how to fish. He had only tasted fish that others gave him. He was eager to learn to catch his own.

"Please Fox, will you tell me how to fish?" asked Bear.

So, the mean old Fox said to Bear, "Cut a hole in the ice and stick your tail in the hole. It will get cold, but soon the fish will begin to bite. When you can stand it no longer, pull your tail out. It will be covered with fish!"

"Will it hurt?" asked Bear, patting his tail.

"It will hurt some," admitted Fox. "But the longer you leave your tail in the water, the more fish you will catch."

Bear did as Fox told him. He loved fish, so he left his tail in the icy water a very, very long time. The ice froze around Bear's tail. When he pulled free, his tail remained stuck in the ice. That is why bears today have short tails.

1. How does Fox get his string of fish? **He stole it.**

2. What does he tell Bear to do? **to put his tail in a hole in the ice to catch fish**

3. Why does Bear do as Fox told him? **He loves to eat fish but doesn't know how to catch them.**

4. How many fish does Bear catch? **none**

5. What happens when Bear tries to pull his tail out? **His tail remains stuck in the ice.**

35

Recognizing Details: "Why Bear Has a Short Tail"

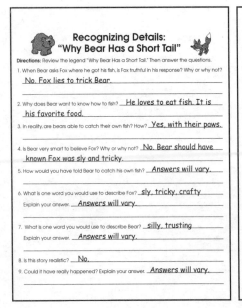

Directions: Review the legend "Why Bear Has a Short Tail." Then answer the questions.

1. When Bear asks Fox where he got his fish, is Fox truthful in his response? Why or why not? **No. Fox lies to trick Bear.**

2. Why does Bear want to know how to fish? **He loves to eat fish. It is his favorite food.**

3. In reality, are bears able to catch their own fish? How? **Yes, with their paws.**

4. Is Bear very smart to believe Fox? Why or why not? **No. Bear should have known Fox was sly and tricky.**

5. How would you have told Bear to catch his own fish? **Answers will vary.**

6. What is one word you would use to describe Fox? **sly, tricky, crafty**

Explain your answer. **Answers will vary.**

7. What is one word you would use to describe Bear? **silly, trusting**

Explain your answer. **Answers will vary.**

8. Is this story realistic? **No.**

9. Could it have really happened? Explain your answer. **Answers will vary.**

36

Predicting: "How the Donkey Got Long Ears"

Directions: Write your predictions to answer these questions.

1. How do you think animals got their names? _____

2. Why would it be confusing if animals _____   *Answers will vary.*

Directions: Read the legend "How the Donkey Got Long Ears." Then answer the questions.

In the beginning when the world was young, animals had no names. It was very confusing! A woman would say, "Tell the thingamajig to bring in the paper." The man would say, "What thingamajig?" She was talking about the dog, of course, but the man didn't know that.

Together, they decided to name the animals on their farm. First, they named their pet thingamajig Dog. They named the pink thingamajig that oinked Pig. They named the red thingamajig that crowed Rooster. They named the white thingamajig that laid eggs Hen. They named the little yellow thingamajigs that cheeped Chicks. They named the big brown thingamajig they rode Horse.

Then they came to another thingamajig. It looked like Horse, but was smaller. It would be confusing to call the smaller thingamajig Horse, they decided.

"Let's name it Donkey," said the woman. So they did.

Soon all the animals knew their names. All but Donkey, that is. Donkey kept forgetting.

"What kind of a thingamajig am I again?" he would ask the man.

"You are Donkey," the man would answer. Each time Donkey forgot, the man tugged on Donkey's ears to help him remember.

Soon, however, Donkey would forget his name again.

"Uh, what's my name?" he would ask the woman.

She would answer, "Donkey! Donkey! Donkey!" and pull his ears each time. She was a clever woman but not very patient.

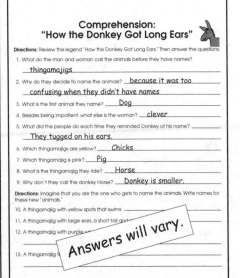

At first, the man and woman did not notice that Donkey's ears grew longer each time they were pulled. Donkey was patient but not very clever. It took him a long time to learn his name. By the time he remembered his name was Donkey, his ears were much longer than Horse's ears. That is why donkeys have long ears.

3. What words could you use to describe Donkey? **forgetful**

Explain your choice. **Answers will vary.**

37

Comprehension: "How the Donkey Got Long Ears"

Directions: Review the legend "How the Donkey Got Long Ears." Then answer the questions.

1. What do the man and woman call the animals before they have names? **thingamajigs**

2. Why do they decide to name the animals? **because it was too confusing when they didn't have names**

3. What is the first animal they name? **Dog**

4. Besides being impatient, what else is the woman? **clever**

5. What did the people do each time they reminded Donkey of his name? **They tugged on his ears.**

6. Which thingamajigs are yellow? **Chicks**

7. Which thingamajig is pink? **Pig**

8. What is the thingamajig they ride? **Horse**

9. Why don't they call the donkey Horse? **Donkey is smaller.**

Directions: Imagine that you are the one who gets to name the animals. Write names for these new "animals."

10. A thingamajig with yellow spots that swims _____

11. A thingamajig with large ears, a short tail and _____

12. A thingamajig with purple _____   *Answers will vary.*

13. A thingamajig _____

38

112

Following Directions: Puzzling Out the Animals

Directions: Review the legend "How the Donkey Got Long Ears." Then work the puzzle.

Across:
3. Is the woman patient?
4. This thingamajig cheeps.
5. This thingamajig lays eggs.
6. Is the woman clever?
7. This thingamajig is pink.

Down:
1. This animal can't remember its name.
2. This is what the animals are called before they have names.
5. People ride this brown animal.

Crossword:
DONKEY (down), TINGAMAJIGS, CHICK, NO, YES, HEN, HORSE, PIGS

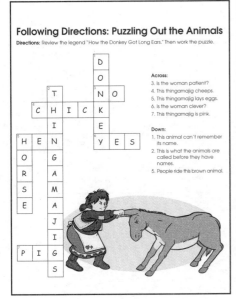

39

Review

Rudyard Kipling wrote many legends explaining such things as why bears have short tails, how the camel got his hump and why a leopard has spots. He wrote his stories in a book called *Just So Stories for Little Children.* You can find a copy of Kipling's book at the library or a bookstore.

Directions: Think about how animals look and behave. Using your wildest imagination, write a short explanation for the following situations.

1. Why the pig has a short tail _____
2. How the elephant got his big ears _____
3. Why birds fly _____
4. Why rabbits are timid _____
5. How the giraffe got a l_____
6. How the mou_____

Directions: Illustrate one____ our stories as a three- or four-panel cartoon.

Answers will vary.

40

Comprehension: "Why Cats and Dogs Fight"

Directions: Read the legend "Why Cats and Dogs Fight." Then answer the questions.

Long ago, Cat and Dog were friends. They played together. They ate together. They even slept near one another.

Yes, Cat and Dog got along very well! The reason was simple. All the other animals had to work for humans. But because Cat was so clean, it did not have to work. And because Dog was so loyal, it did not have to work either. Cat and Dog were the only animals who had time to play. They enjoyed themselves very much.

Everything was too good to be true! Cat and Dog wanted to make sure their lives stayed easy. They asked the old man and woman who owned them to sign a paper saying they would never have to work. That way, they would have proof that they could spend their lives at play.

The old man and woman signed the paper. Then Dog buried it in the ground with his bones. After their masters died, the other animals grew more and more jealous.

"The people aren't here any more to protect them. Why should they get off so easy?" Ox asked Cow.

"You're right," said Cow. "Let's find that paper and destroy it. Then there will be no proof that Cat and Dog can play. They will have to work like we do."

Ox and Cow looked everywhere, but they could not find the paper. Finally, they asked Rat to help. Rat sniffed and sniffed. At last, he smelled the paper. He pulled it from the ground and gave it to Ox. Ox ground it under his hoof and destroyed it. Then Dog had to go to work as a hunter. Cat had to catch mice. Cat never forgave Dog for burying the paper in a spot where Rat could find. To this day, that's why cats and dogs fight.

1. Why didn't Cat have to work? **Cat was so clean.**
2. Why didn't Dog have to work? **Dog was so loyal.**
3. What animals talk about finding the paper? **Ox and Cow**
4. Who destroys the paper? **Ox**
5. Who finds the paper? **Rat**

41

Comprehension: "Why Cats and Dogs Fight"

Directions: Review the legend "Why Cats and Dogs Fight." Then answer the questions.

1. What do Cat and Dog do to make sure their life stays easy? **They make their owners sign a paper saying they would never have to work.**
2. Does their plan work? **No.**
3. Why not? **The other animals were jealous.**
4. When does the easy time stop for the cat c **when Ox destroys the paper**
5. Cat gets mad at Dog for burying the paper in a place where Rat can easily find it. Do you think Dog also gets mad at Cat? Explain your answer.
6. What other animal pair could you compa____
7. Why did you select this animal pair?
8. Does the quarreling of Dog and ____ animals remind you of your own quarrels with your brothers or ____
9. What if Rat____ er? Rewrite the end of the story, beginning with these words: "Rat____ why cats and dogs …"

Answers will vary.

42

Main Idea: "The Sly Fox"

Directions: Read the legend "The Sly Fox." Then answer the questions.

One evening, Fox met Wolf in the forest. Wolf was in a terrible mood. He felt hungry, too. So he said to Fox, "Don't move! I'm going to eat you this minute."

As he spoke, Wolf backed Fox up against a tree. Fox realized she couldn't run away. "I will have to use my wits instead of my legs," she thought to herself.

Aloud to Wolf, Fox said calmly, "I would have made a good dinner for you last year. But I've had three little babies since then. I spend all my time looking for food to feed them."

Before she could go on, Wolf interrupted. "I don't care how many children you have! I'm going to eat you right now." Wolf began closing in on Fox.

"Stop!" shouted Fox. "Look how skinny I am. I ran off all my fat looking for food for my children. But I know where you can find something that's good and fat!" Wolf backed off to listen.

"There's a well near here. In the bottom of it is a big fat piece of cheese. I don't like cheese, so it's of no use to me. Come, I'll show you."

Wolf trotted off after Fox, making sure she could not run away.

"See," said Fox when they got to the well.

Inside was what looked like a round yellow piece of cheese. It was really the moon's reflection, but Wolf didn't know this. Wolf leaned over the well, wondering how to get the cheese. Fox jumped up quickly and pushed Wolf in.

"I am a sly, old thing," Fox chuckled as she trotted home to her children. And to this day, that's why foxes are sly.

1. What is the main idea of this legend? (Check one.)
   ✓ Fox is cornered but uses her wits to outsmart Wolf and save her own life.
   ___ Wolf is in a terrible mood and wants to eat Fox.
   ___ Wolf thinks the moon was made of cheese.

2. Why did Fox say she will not make a good meal for Wolf? **She was too thin because she spent all her time searching for food for her babies.**

3. What happens to Wolf at the end? **Fox pushes Wolf into the well.**

43

Recognizing Details: "The Sly Fox"

Directions: Review the legend "The Sly Fox." Then answer the questions.

1. What are three events in the story that show Wolf's bad mood? **Answers will vary.**
2. What does Fox say she will have to use to get away from Wolf? **her wits**
3. Where does Fox tell Wolf he can find a nice fat meal? **at the bottom of the well**
4. How does Fox finally rid herself of Wolf? **She pushes him into the well.**
5. What does Fox say as she trots home? **"I am a sly old thing."**
6. Have you ever been in a situation where you used words to solve a problem instead of fighting with someone? Write about it.
7. In addition to teaching why foxes are sly, wh____ this story teach?

Answers will vary.

44

Comprehension: "King of the Beasts"

Directions: Read the legend "King of the Beasts." Then answer the questions.

Once, a shy little rabbit was sleeping under a palm tree. Suddenly, a coconut fell and startled the rabbit awake. The rabbit began to twitch and worry.

"What was that awful noise?" he said. He looked around but didn't see the coconut. "The Earth must be breaking apart. Oh dear, oh dear, oh dear."

The little rabbit began running in circles. Soon a monkey joined him.

"Why are you running?" the monkey asked, trotting along beside the rabbit.

"The Earth is breaking apart, and I'm trying to escape," panted the little rabbit.

They were joined by a deer, a fox and an elephant. When they heard the Earth was breaking up, they all followed the rabbit. Soon a huge herd of animals was running in a circle.

"What's going on?" roared the lion to the elephant when he saw the herd.

"The Earth is breaking up!" shouted the elephant. "We are trying to escape."

The lion looked around. Except for all the dust, everything looked fine.

"Who said the Earth is breaking up?" he roared back to the elephant.

"The fox told me!" the elephant replied.

The lion asked the fox, and the fox said the deer told him. The deer said the monkey had told him. Finally, the lion traced the story to the rabbit.

"Show me the place!" the lion demanded.

The rabbit led the lion back to the palm tree. Right away, the lion saw the coconut on the ground.

"Silly rabbit!" he roared. "What you heard was a coconut falling. Go and tell the other animals they are safe."

The rabbit rushed to tell the other animals. They stopped running.

"The lion is smart!" said the monkey. "Let's name him 'King of the Beasts.'" So they did.

1. What kind of tree is the rabbit sleeping under? __a palm tree__

2. Why does he think the Earth is breaking up? __A coconut fell and startled__ __him awake.__

3. Which animal is the first to join the rabbit? __monkey__

4. What does the lion call the rabbit? __"silly rabbit"__

5. Who suggests naming the lion "King of the Beasts"? __monkey__

45

Comprehension: "King of the Beasts"

Directions: Review the legend "King of the Beasts." Then answer the questions.

1. How does the lion become "King of the Beasts"? __He discovers that the__ __Earth is not breaking apart.__

2. Instead of panicking about the Earth breaking apart, what should the rabbit have done? __He could have looked to see what made the loud noise.__

3. Instead of following the rabbit around in a circle, what should the monkey, deer and fox have done?

4. Do you think naming the lion "King of the ___ ___" ... dea? Why or why not?

5. What does this story te... ___ ...ressure? Explain.

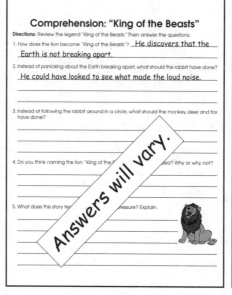

Answers will vary.

46

Recognizing Details: "Lazy Sheep"

Directions: Read the poem about the lazy sheep. Then answer the questions.

"Lazy sheep, please tell me why
In the grassy field you lie?
You eat and sleep away your day
While people work and sweat for pay!"
"Boy, do not talk to me so mean!"
Replied the sheep, so white he gleamed.
"I'm busy growing wool that's new
To spin into some clothes for you!"
The boy looked sad, his face got red.
"I'm sorry for the things I said!"

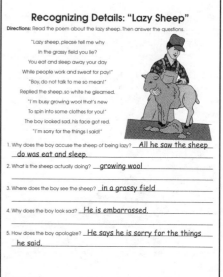

1. Why does the boy accuse the sheep of being lazy? __All he saw the sheep__ __do was eat and sleep.__

2. What is the sheep actually doing? __growing wool__

3. Where does the boy see the sheep? __in a grassy field__

4. Why does the boy look sad? __He is embarrassed.__

5. How does the boy apologize? __He says he is sorry for the things__ __he said.__

47

Main Idea: "The Mouse"

Directions: Read the story "The Mouse." Then answer the questions.

One day when the cat and mouse were playing, the cat bit off the mouse's tail.

"Ouch!" cried the mouse. "Give me back my tail this instant!"

"I'll give your tail back when you go to the cow and bring me some milk!" replied the cat.

She held the mouse's tail high so the mouse could not reach it.

Right away, the mouse went to ask the cow for milk.

"I'll give you milk if you go to the farmer and get me some hay," said the cow.

When the mouse asked the farmer for hay, he said: "I'll give you hay if you go to the butcher and get me some meat."

The mouse wanted her tail back, so she went to the butcher. "I'll give you meat if you go to the baker and bring me some bread," said the butcher.

The mouse went to the baker, who said, "I'll give you bread. But if you get into my grain, I'll cut off your head!" The mouse quickly promised never to get into the baker's grain.

Then the baker gave the mouse bread. The mouse gave the bread to the butcher and the butcher gave the mouse meat. The mouse gave the meat to the farmer and the farmer gave the mouse hay. The mouse gave the hay to the cow and the cow gave the mouse milk. The mouse gave the cat milk and—finally!—the mouse got her tail back!

1. The main idea is: (Check one.)

__✓__ To get what you want, you must be persistent.

_____ A mouse's tail is worth a lot of work to a mouse.

_____ Everybody is greedy, especially the baker.

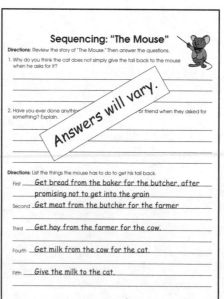

2. What does the mouse promise the baker never to get into? __his grain__

Directions: Fill in the blanks to show the steps the mouse follows to get her tail back.

3. She gets bread from the baker and gives it to __the butcher__

4. She gets meat from the butcher and gives it to __the farmer__

5. She gets hay from the farmer and gives it to __the cow__

6. She gets milk from the cow and gives it to __the cat__

7. That's when she __gets her tail back__

48

Sequencing: "The Mouse"

Directions: Review the story of "The Mouse." Then answer the questions.

1. Why do you think the cat does not simply give the tail back to the mouse when he asks for it?

2. Have you ever done anythin... ___ ...or friend when they asked for something? Explain.

Answers will vary.

Directions: List the things the mouse has to do to get its tail back.

First __Get bread from the baker for the butcher, after__ __promising not to get into the grain__

Second __Get meat from the butcher for the farmer__

Third __Get hay from the farmer for the cow.__

Fourth __Get milk from the cow for the cat.__

Fifth __Give the milk to the cat.__

49

Review

Directions: Review the fables and legends you read. Then write your answers.

1. Explain how "The Mouse" and "The Sly Fox" are similar stories.

2. Explain how "King of the Beasts" and "The Sheep" are ___

3. Compare and contrast the rabbit t___

4. Compare and c___ ...d with one animal fable.

5. Rea___ ...ust So Stories. Write your reaction to the story.

Answers will vary.

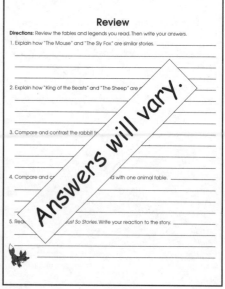

50

Animal Legend Organizer

Directions: Follow the instructions to write a legend of your own.

1. Select one of the following titles for your legend. Circle the one you plan to use.

How the Tiger Got Stripes	How the Elephant Got a Tusk
How the Giraffe Got a Long Neck	How the Kangaroo Got Her Pouch
How the Gazelle Got Twisty Horns	Why the Pig Has a Short Tail
How the Elephant Got Big Ears	Why Birds Fly
Why Rabbits Are Timid	How the Giraffe Got a Long Neck
How the Mouse Got a Long Tail	Why Fish Swim

2. Briefly explain the type of conflict that will be in your legend. _____

_____

3. Write words and phrases to show events you pl_____ legend.

_____

4. Summarize how you plan to settle _____ the problem.

Answers will vary.

Directions: Write your _____ illustrate it if you like.

_____

51

Recognizing Details: Giraffes

Directions: Read about giraffes. Then answer the questions.

Giraffes are tall, beautiful, graceful animals that live in Africa. When they are grown, male giraffes are about 18 feet tall. Adult females are about 14 feet tall.

Giraffes are not fat animals, but because they are so big, they weigh a lot. The average male weighs 2,800 pounds. Females weigh about 400 pounds less. Giraffes reach their full height when they are four years old. They continue to gain weight until they are about eight years old.

If you have ever seen giraffes, you know their necks and legs are very long. They are not awkward, though! Giraffes can move very quickly. They like to jump over fences and streams. They do this gracefully. They do not trip over their long legs.

If they are frightened, they can run 35 miles an hour. When giraffes gallop, all four feet are sometimes off the ground! Usually, young and old giraffes pace along at about 10 miles an hour.

Giraffes are strong. They can use their back legs as weapons. A lion can run faster than a giraffe, but a giraffe can kill a lion with one quick kick from its back legs.

Giraffes do not look scary. Their long eyelashes make them look gentle. They usually have a curious look on their faces. Many people think they are cute. Do you?

1. What is the weight of a full-grown male giraffe? __2,800 pounds__
2. What is the weight of an adult female? __2,400 pounds__
3. When does a giraffe run 35 miles an hour? __when it is frightened__
4. What do giraffes use as weapons? __their back legs__
5. For how long do giraffes continue to gain weight?
__until they are 8 years old__
6. When do giraffes reach their full height?
__when they are 4 years old__
7. Use a dictionary. What does **gallop** mean?
__to run quickly; to run at full speed__

52

Comprehension: More About Giraffes

Directions: Read more about giraffes. Then answer the questions.

Most people don't notice, but giraffes have different patterns of spots. Certain species of giraffes have small spots. Other species have large spots. Some species have spots that are very regular. You can tell where one spot ends and another begins. Other species have spots that are kind of blotchy. This means the spots are not set off from each other as clearly. There are many other kinds of spot patterns. The pattern of a giraffe's spots is called "markings." No two giraffes have exactly the same markings.

There is one very rare type of giraffe. It is totally black! Have you ever seen one? This kind of giraffe is called a melanistic (mell-an-iss-tick) giraffe. The name comes from the word "melanin," which is the substance in cells that gives them color. Giraffes' spots help them blend in with their surroundings. A black giraffe would not blend in well with tree trunks and leaves. Maybe that is why they are so rare.

Being able to blend with surroundings helps giraffes survive. If a lion can't see a giraffe, he certainly can't eat it. This is called "protective coloration." The animal's color helps protect it.

Another protection giraffes have is their keen eyesight. Their large eyes are on the sides of their heads. Giraffes see anything that moves! They can see another animal a mile away! It is very hard to sneak up on a giraffe. Those who try usually get a quick kick with a powerful back leg.

1. What are markings? __the pattern of an animal's spots__
2. How far away can a giraffe see another animal? __one mile__
3. Where are a giraffe's eyes? __on the sides of its head__
4. What is protective colorat __being able to blend into the surroundings__
5. What color is the very rare type of giraffe? __black__
6. How do giraffes protect themselves? __They kick with their back legs.__
7. How many kinds of spot patterns do giraffes have? ☐ two ☐ four ☑ many
8. Use a dictionary. What does **species** mean? __a group of animals closely__
__related and capable of breeding with others in the same__
__species__

53

Following Directions: Puzzling Out Giraffes

Directions: Review what you read about giraffes. Read more about giraffes below. Then work the puzzle.

Have you noticed that giraffes have a curious look? That is because they are always paying attention. Their lives depend upon it! Giraffes cannot save themselves from a lion if they don't see it. Giraffes look around a lot. Even when they are chewing their food, they are checking to see if danger is near.

By nature, giraffes are gentle. They do not attack unless they are in danger. A giraffe will lower its head when it is angry. It will open its nostrils and its mouth. Then watch out!

Crossword with answers: MARKINGS, ANGRY, CURIOUS, SPECIES, GENTLE, COLORATION, AFRICA, AWAY, MELANISTIC

Across:
2. How a giraffe feels when it lowers its head and opens its nose and mouth.
4. Giraffes look this way because they are always paying attention.
6. By nature, giraffes are _____.
7. The continent where giraffes live.
9. Another name for a black giraffe is _____.

Down:
1. The patterns of a giraffe's spots.
3. An animal's ability to blend with surroundings is called protective _____.
5. _____ means a certain kind of animal.
8. Giraffes' eyes are so keen they can see another animal a mile _____.
10. Are giraffes often mean?

54

Recognizing Details: Giraffes

Directions: Review what you learned about giraffes. Then answer the questions.

1. How are a giraffe's spots helpful? __They help them blend in__
__with their surroundings.__
2. Is it easy to sneak up on a giraffe? Why not? __No, because they are always__
__paying attention and can see a long ways.__
3. What makes a giraffe look so gentle? __They have long eyelashes.__
4. How do you know when a giraffe is angry? __It will lower its head and__
__open its nostrils and mouth.__
5. Do you think a giraffe in a zoo is as observant as a giraffe in the wilds of Africa? Why or why not?
__Answers will vary.__
6. Do you think giraffes have any other enemies besides lions? __Yes__
What animals might they be? __Answers may include: hyenas,__
__cheetahs__
7. Why do you suppose giraffes grow so large? __Answers will vary.__
8. Use a dictionary. What does **habitat** mean? Describe the giraffe's natural habitat.
__Habitat is a place where an animal lives in its natural__
__state. Giraffes live on open grassy plains and sometimes__
__near trees.__

55

Comprehension: Wild Horses

Directions: Read about wild horses. Then answer the questions.

Have you ever heard of a car called a Mustang? It is named after a type of wild horse.

In the 1600s, the Spanish explorers who came to North America brought horses with them. Some of these horses escaped onto the prairies and plains. With no one to feed them or ride them, they became wild. Their numbers quickly grew, and they roamed in herds. They ran free and ate grass on the prairie.

Later, when the West was settled, people needed horses. They captured wild ones. This was not easy to do. Wild horses could run very fast. They did not want to be captured! These men were called "mustangers." Can you guess why?

After cars were invented, people did not need as many horses. Not as many mustangers were needed to catch them. More and more wild horses roamed the western prairies. In 1925, about a million mustangs were running loose.

The government was worried that the herds would eat too much grass. Ranchers who owned big herds of cattle complained that their animals didn't have enough to eat because the mustangs ate all the grass. Permission was given to ranchers and others to kill many of the horses. Thousands were killed and sold to companies that made them into pet food.

Now, wild horses live in only 12 states. The largest herds are in California, New Mexico, Oregon, Wyoming and Nevada. Most people who live in these states never see wild horses. The herds live away from people in the distant plains and mountains. They are safer there.

1. What is one type of wild horse called? __a mustang__
2. What were men called who captured wild horses? __mustangers__
3. About how many wild horses were running free in the U.S. in 1925? __one million__
4. The wild mustangs were killed and turned into ☐ cars. ☑ pet food. ☐ lunch meat.
5. The largest herds of wild horses are now in

☑ Oregon. ☐ Ohio. ☑ New Mexico. ☑ Wyoming.
☑ California. ☑ Nevada. ☐ Kansas. ☐ Arkansas.

56

Main Idea: More About Wild Horses

Directions: Read more about wild horses. Then answer the questions.

Have you noticed that in any large group, one person seems to be the leader? This is true for wild horses, too. The leader of a band of wild horses is a stallion. Stallions are adult male horses.

The stallion's job is important. He watches out for danger. If a bear or other animal comes close, he lets out a warning cry. This helps keep the other horses safe. Sometimes they all run away together. Other times, the stallion protects the other horses. He shows his teeth. He rears up on his back legs. Often, he scares the other animal away. Then the horses can safely continue eating grass.

Much of the grass on the prairies is gone now. Wild horses must move around a lot to find new grass. They spend about half their time eating and looking for food. If they cannot find prairie grass, wild horses will eat tree bark. They will eat flowers. If they can't find these either, wild horses will eat anything that grows!

Wild horses also need plenty of water. It is often hot in the places where they roam. At least twice a day, they find streams and take long, long drinks. Like people, wild horses lose water when they sweat. They run and sweat a lot in hot weather. To survive, they need as much water as they can get.

Wild horses also use water another way. When they find deep water, they wade into it. It feels good! It cools their skin.

1. What is the main idea? (Check one.)
   ____ Wild horses need plenty of water.
   ✓ Wild horses move in bands protected by a stallion.
   ____ Wild horses eat grass.

2. What are two reasons why wild horses need water? _to drink and to cool their skin_

3. Why do wild horses move around so much? _to find new grass_

4. What do wild horses most like to eat? _prairie grass_

5. What do wild horses spend half their time doing? _eating and looking for food_

57

Recognizing Details: Wild Horses

Directions: Review what you read about wild horses. Then answer the questions.

1. How did horses come to North America and become wild? _Spanish explorers brought them. Some escaped and became wild._

2. Why is it so difficult to capture, tame and train wild horses? _Wild horses can run very fast and do not want to be captured._

3. Do you think it was right of the government to allow ____ing of wild horses?
   Explain your answer. _____

4. Do you think the remaining ____ protected?
   Explain your answer.

Answers will vary.

5. What is the role of the lead stallion in a wild horse herd? _to watch out for danger and protect the herd_

6. What are some things wild horses have in common with giraffes? _____

7. What do you think will happen ____ prairie lands continue to disappear as a result of development ____ sses?

Answers will vary.

58

Comprehension: Sea Lions

Directions: Read about sea lions. Then answer the questions.

Sea lions are friendly-looking animals. Their round faces and whiskers remind people of the faces of small dogs. The almond shape of their eyes gives them a look of intelligence. Whether it is true or not, sea lions often look as though they are thinking.

Sea lions behave like playful children. They push each other off rocks. They slide into the water. Sometimes they body surf! Like people, they often ride the crest of waves. They let the waves carry them near the shore. Then they swim back out to ride more waves.

Although sea lions do not have real toys, they like to play with seaweed. They toss it in the air. They catch it in their mouths. Yuck! They must not mind the taste!

If you have been to a marine park, you may have watched sea lions. Sea lions can be taught many tricks. They can balance balls on their noses. They can jump through hoops. Their trainers give them fish to reward them for doing tricks. Sea lions look very pleased with themselves when they perform. They love fish, and they grow to love applause.

1. What are three ways sea lions play? _They push each other off rocks, slide into the water, body surf and play with seaweed._

2. Why do sea lions look intelligent? _They have almond-shaped eyes._

3. What tricks can sea lions be taught to do? _balance balls on their noses, jump through hoops_

4. As a reward, trainers give sea lions
   ✓ fish.   ☐ hugs.   ☐ applause.

59

Recognizing Details: More About Sea Lions

Directions: Read more about sea lions. Then answer the questions.

Sea lions love water! That is a good thing, because they spend most of their lives in it. Usually, the water is very cold. People cannot stay in cold water very long. The coldness slows down a person's heartbeat. It can actually make a person's heart stop beating.

Sea lions do not feel the cold. Their bodies are covered with a special layer of fat called blubber. The blubber is like a thick coat. It keeps the sea lion's body heat in. It keeps the bone-chilling cold out.

Like people, sea lions are mammals. They have warm blood. They breathe air. Baby sea lions are born on land. Like human mothers, the mother sea lions produce milk for their babies. Like human babies, sea lions snuggle up with their mothers when they nurse. The mother knows just what her baby smells like. This is how she tells which baby is hers. She will only nurse her own baby.

Baby sea lions are called pups. Female sea lions are called cows. Male sea lions are called bulls. When pups are a few days old, their mothers leave them for a while each day. They go into the ocean to hunt fish. The pups don't seem to mind. They gather together in small groups called pods. The pods are like a nursery school. But no teacher is in charge. As many as 200 pups may spend the day together playing, swimming and sleeping.

1. What are male, female and baby sea lions called? _male — bulls, females — cows, babies — pups_

2. How do sea lions stay warm in cold water? _Their bodies are covered with a layer of fat, called blubber._

3. When do cows begin to leave their p____ _when the pups are a few days old_

4. Where do the cows go? _into the ocean to hunt fish_

5. What are small groups of pups called? _pods_

6. How can a cow tell which pup is hers? _by its smell_

60

Main Idea: Pupping Time

Directions: Read about sea lion "pupping time." Then answer the questions.

When sea lion cows gather on the beach to give birth, it is called "pupping time." Pupping time is never a surprise. It always occurs in June. Thousands of sea lions may gather in one spot for pupping time. It is sort of like one big birthday party.

The cow stays with her pups for about a week after birth. During that time, she never leaves her baby. If she must go somewhere, she drags her pup along. She grabs the loose skin around her pup's neck with her teeth. To humans, it doesn't look comfortable, but it doesn't hurt the pup.

One place the mother must go is to the water. Because of her blubber, she gets hot on land. To cool off, she takes a dip in the ocean. When she comes out, she sniffs her pup to make sure she's got the right baby. Then she drags him back again to a spot she has staked out. After a week of being dragged around, do you think the pup is ready to play?

1. Why do thousands of sea lions gather together at a certain time? _to give birth at pupping time_

2. Why isn't pupping time ever a surprise? _it happens every June_

3. How does a cow take her pup along when she goes for a cool dip?
   First, grab _the loose skin at the pup's neck with her teeth_
   Then, _drag it along_
   After the swim, sniff _the pup to be sure she's got the right pup_

4. What is the main idea? (Check one.)
   ✓ Thousands of cows gather at pupping time to give birth and afterwards stay with their pups for a week.
   ____ Thousands of sea lions take cools dips and usually drag their pups along.
   ____ Pups are born in June.

61

Comprehension: Sea Lions

Directions: Review what you read about sea lions. Then answer the questions.

1. What makes sea lions so friendly looking? _their round faces and whiskers_

2. How are people like sea lions? _Answers may include: They both like to play in the water._

3. Pretend you are a pup in a pod. What would your day be like? What would you do?
   Answers will vary.

4. Why do sea lions go into the water so much? _to cool off and to hunt for food_

5. How do you think sea lions protect themselves?

6. What is the sea lion's habitat like?

Answers will vary.

62

Review

Directions: Follow the instructions. Write your answers.

1. Create a wild animal alphabet and illustrate it on drawing paper.

Example:
A — ALLIGATOR
B — BEAR
C — CROCODILE

2. Select one of the wild animals you read about. Make a diorama of its habitat. A **diorama** is a three-dimensional model of a scene.

3. Compare the giraffe, wild horse and sea lion. ___ three animals are alike and the ways they are different.

	Giraffe		Seal Lions
Alike			
Different			

Answers will vary.

4. What physical charact___ animals help them survive. Which do you think is the best and why?

5. How do these animal stories differ from the animal legends and fables you read?
These are nonfiction—facts about real animals. Legends and fables are fiction.

63

Recognizing Details: Pet Rabbits

Directions: Read about pet rabbits. Then answer the questions.

Rabbits come in many colors, and their fur has many patterns. The Dutch rabbit has white in the front of its body and brown on the back. Its ears are brown, too, and it has a brown "mask" over its eyes. Its front legs are white and its back legs are brown. The tips of the toes on its back legs are white.

People think Dutch rabbits are adorable! They look like stuffed toys and weigh about five pounds when fully grown. The rabbit is called "Dutch," but it was first bred in Belgium.

Another popular rabbit is the Californian. Can you guess where it was first bred? It is a fat white rabbit with pink eyes. The Californian rabbit has touches of light brown on its toes and nose. Its ears are light brown also.

Did you know some people raise rabbits for their fur? The fur from the Angora rabbit is actually called wool. There are 13 colors of Angora rabbit, but white is the most popular. This rabbit has long hair and pink eyes. It can grow to weigh six pounds. Because its fur is long, it must be groomed every day. To "groom" an animal means to comb and care for its fur.

Some breeds of rabbits are called giants. Compared to other rabbits, they really are big. The Belgian hare, a reddish-colored rabbit, can weigh up to 9 pounds. Other breeds are called dwarfs. Dwarfs are very small. Fully grown, they weigh only about 2 pounds. A popular dwarf rabbit is the Netherland. Most Netherland rabbits are white with pink eyes.

1. How many breeds of rabbits are named in the article? __5__
2. What are the names of the breeds? __Dutch, Californian, Angora__ __Belgian, Netherland__
3. What is one type of giant rabbit? __Belgian hare__
4. What is one type of dwarf rabbit? __Netherland__
5. How much does a Belgian hare weigh? __up to 9 pounds__
6. How much does a Dutch rabbit weigh? __about 5 pounds__
7. Use a reference source. What is the difference between a hare and a rabbit?
__Answers will vary.__

64

Comprehension: Caring for Pet Rabbits

Directions: Read about caring for pet rabbits. Then answer the questions.

Most pet rabbits live outside in special homes, called hutches. Rabbit hutches are small and have wire on the sides and bottom to let air in. The wire on the bottom also lets the animals' droppings fall through. This helps keep their hutch clean.

Pet rabbits need exercise, too. They do not like being caged all the time. Would you? That is why pet owners build "rabbit runs" for their pets. Rabbit runs are much bigger and longer than cages. They do not have floors. They fit over the grass. Put the rabbit inside the run and guess what it does?

Some people let their rabbits run free for exercise. But you must take care that the rabbit does not run away. Only let the rabbit free if your yard is fenced. Also, you need to protect your pet from dogs and other animals.

Of course, you should pet your rabbit. To pick it up, put one hand on the back of the rabbit's neck. This area of loose skin is called the "scruff." Put your other hand under the rabbit's rear end. Then lift the rabbit slowly and firmly. Rabbits do not like fast movements. That's why you should never grab your rabbit. Also, never, never pick up your rabbit by its ears.

Hold your rabbit close to your chest. This makes the rabbit feel secure. It also keeps it from falling. Put your hand under its back legs. Hold the legs firmly so your rabbit cannot kick. Then gently scratch its fur. Rabbits cannot purr, but you can tell when your pet is happy.

1. What do pet owners build for their rabbits to exercise in? __rabbit runs__
2. What is the difference between a hutch and a rabbit run? __Rabbit runs are__ __longer, bigger and don't have floors.__
3. What is the rabbit's "scruff"? __loose skin at back of neck__
4. Never pick your rabbit up by its
   - [ ] scruff.
   - [x] ears.
   - [ ] body.
5. After you pick up your rabbit, hold it close to your
   - [x] chest.
   - [ ] face.
   - [ ] arms.
6. Hold your rabbit's legs firmly so it cannot
   - [ ] purr.
   - [ ] cry.
   - [x] kick.

65

Following Directions: Rabbit Food

Directions: Read about what rabbits eat. Then work the puzzle.

Many people think rabbits only eat lettuce. They do like lettuce, but it's not the only thing rabbits eat.

Rabbits also need protein. Most pet owners supply this with dry rabbit food. The food is called pellets. Rabbits should eat twice a day. They also need fresh water every day. Besides lettuce, they like carrots, cabbage and turnips. These vegetables are called greens. Rabbits like them mixed together.

Pet rabbits will eat wild plants. They like dandelion leaves and blackberry leaves. They also like a kind of plant called chickweed. Learn what these plants look like. Then pick them for your rabbit. Some plants are poisonous. For example, buttercups can kill rabbits. So can poppy flowers. If you gather wild plants, be very careful.

Crossword puzzle:
F - PROTEIN (across)
- L - TURNIPS
- O - WILD
- E - CABBAGE
- CARROTS

Across:
3. Pet owners feed their rabbits this in pellets.
4. A vegetable pet rabbits will eat
5. Rabbits also will eat _____ plants.
6. This vegetable is like lettuce. Rabbits like it.
7. Another vegetable rabbits like

Down:
1. Rabbits like this, but it is not the only food they like.
2. A plant that will poison a rabbit is the poppy _____.
3. Pet rabbits get their protein in these.

66

Comprehension: Baby Rabbits

Directions: Read about baby rabbits. Then answer the questions.

Many people think newborn animals are cute. Baby rabbits grow inside their mothers for only 31 days before they are born. They complete a lot of their development outside the mother. When they are born, they have no fur. They look like little rats! Would you call newborn rabbits cute?

The babies are blind, and they don't open their eyes until they are 10 days old. At the beginning, they can only feel their mother. They cannot see her.

When they are first born, baby rabbits are very delicate. It could hurt them if you picked them up. Do not touch them until they are at least 3 weeks old. By then, they will have fur. Their eyes will be open. Their ears will be standing up. They will finally look like rabbits!

Even though they are much stronger after three weeks, do not hold them long. Their mother will not like it. Like most mothers, she feels a strong need to protect her babies. Also, they are still nursing. This means they are drinking her milk. They need her milk to grow stronger, and that is another reason not to hold them. That is why you should not hold the babies very long.

By the time they are 6 weeks old, baby rabbits are active. They can eat food other than their mother's milk. When they are 8 weeks old, you can move them into their own hutch. They do not need their mother anymore to survive. They are still growing, though. Adult rabbits need only two meals a day. Baby rabbits need three meals a day until they are 3 months old.

1. How long does the baby rabbit grow inside the mother? __31 days__
2. When do baby rabbits open their eyes? __after 10 days__
3. Why is it unwise to handle newborn rabbits? __They are very delicate.__ __They need to nurse often.__
4. Baby rabbits are active by the time they have lived how many weeks? __6 weeks__
5. You can pick up baby rabbits when they are how many weeks old? __3 weeks__
6. Baby rabbits can move into their own hutch when they are how many weeks old? __8__

67

Comprehension: Rabbits

Directions: Review what you learned about rabbits as pets. Then answer the questions.

1. How do baby rabbits look when they are first born? __They have no fur and__ __look like little rats.__
2. Discuss uses of rabbit fur, especially Angora. __Answers will vary.__
3. Angora wool comes in 13 colors. What do you think they are? __Answers will vary.__
4. Why do many people think rabbits are cute? __They look soft and cuddly.__
5. The article mentioned several reasons why you need to be extremely careful with a baby rabbit. Write an explanation for each one. __Answers will vary.__
6. What makes a rabbit feel secure? __Baby rabbits need their mothers.__ __Pet rabbits should be held firmly, close to your chest.__
7. Would you like a pet rabbit? ___ Why or why not? ___ __Answers will vary.__

68

Main Idea: Pet Snakes

Directions: Read about pet snakes. Then answer the questions.

Having a snake for a pet is considered very strange by some people! Snakes can be good pets. They are not cuddly like kittens. Like fish, snakes are interesting to watch.

Many people are afraid of snakes. They do not know much about them. One important fact about snakes is that most of them are not poisonous. Only four types of poisonous snakes live in the United States.

People who keep snakes as pets usually put them in cages. The snake must fit comfortably inside. Many snake owners put their pets in empty fish tanks. The snakes like the smooth glass. The owner can see exactly what the snake is doing. You can also put a snake in a wooden cage, but make sure the wood is sanded smooth. Otherwise, it can hurt the snake's skin.

You need to line a snake's cage with newspaper or sand. You will need to change the bedding two or three times each week.

Snakes like privacy. Put a large rock inside your pet's cage. The snake will coil around it. A large log is also good "snake furniture." The snake will crawl up on its "sofa" when it wants to relax.

Some snakes like to wet their skins. Put a big bowl of water in the cage. The bowl should be heavy so the snake can't tip it over. Then the snake can get into its bowl and soak for a while. This makes a good bath for a snake!

1. What is the main idea? (Check one.)

___ Many people are afraid of snakes, but they shouldn't be afraid.
___ There are only four kinds of poisonous snakes in the United States.
___ Snakes like to crawl.
_✓_ Snakes are interesting to watch and can make good pets for certain people. Like other pets, they require care.

2. Why do snakes make good pets for some people? __They are interesting to watch.__

3. Why should you put a rock inside a pet snake's cage? __For privacy, the snack will coil around it.__

4. How often should you change the bedding in a pet snake? __2-3 times per week__

69

Main Idea: Snakes

Directions: Read about snakes. Then answer the questions.

Snakes are **reptiles**. This means they are cold-blooded (their body temperature changes with the surrounding temperature). they lay eggs and their bodies are covered with scales. Many people think the scales are slimey, but they're not. Snakes have smooth, dry skin.

When baby snakes hatch, they are very small. They eat insects and worms. Some kinds of snakes never get very big, and they eat insects and worms all of their lives. Some kinds of snakes, however, can get quite large. The python in Africa can grow to be more than 20 feet long!

Bigger snakes need to eat bigger food. These snakes eat animals like mice, rats or even rabbits and frogs. Some farmers like to see snakes around their barns because snakes eat the rodents that get into the grain.

When snakes grow, their skin doesn't grow with them. They have to shed their skin. The old skin loosens up all over the snake's body, and the snake rubs against rough surfaces like trees and rocks to make it come off. During this time, the snake is blind. If you have a pet snake that is shedding, watch out! Since it can't see, it might think your hand is food and try to bite it. It is best to leave snakes alone when they are shedding. When the snake is done shedding, it can see again, and it has a nice new skin.

1. What is the main idea? (Check one.)

_3_ Different snakes eat different kinds of foods, but they all shed their skins as they grow.
___ Snakes eat insects and worms after they hatch.
___ Farmers like snakes because they shed their skins.

2. What is a reptile? __a cold-blooded animal that lays eggs and is covered with scales__

3. How big can some snakes grow to be? __20 feet__

4. Using context clues, write the definition of the word **rodent**? __animals like mice and rats__

70

Recognizing Details: Snakes

Directions: Review what you learned about snakes. Then answer the questions.

1. Why is having a pet snake considered strange?

2. Do you agree with this? Why or wh___

3. Are you afraid of sn___

Answers will vary.

4. How is caring for a rabbit like caring for a snake? __Both need to be fed and watered. Both need care and a clean cage.__

5. How is it different? __They eat different kinds of food. Rabbits need more exercise. Snakes need "furniture."__

6. How do snakes shed their skins? __The old skin loosens, then they rub against rough surfaces to make it come off.__

7. What does "cold-blooded" mean? __body temperature changes with surrounding temperature__

8. What are some other animals that are cold-blooded? __Answers may include: crocodiles, frogs__

71

Review

Directions: Review what you learned about animals as pets. Then answer the questions.

1. What other types of animals are common pets?

2. Do the animals listed in your answer above require much care? Explain.

3. Do you have a pet? Who___ Explain how you care for it.

4. If you do not have a pet, w___ your parents convincing them you could care for one.

5. What an___ makes the best pet? Explain.

Answers will vary.

72

Recognizing Details: Going to Camp

Directions: Read about going to camp. Then answer the questions.

Have you ever gone to camp? If so, you know you need to pack many things. Usually, the people who run the camp will send a list of what you need to bring. What you need depends on the type of camp and how long you will stay.

If you go to camp for one week, you will probably need the following items. Pack them all in a suitcase or gym bag—if they will fit!

1 bathing suit	5 pairs of shorts	1 pair of sneakers
2 sweaters or sweatshirts	1 jacket	2 pairs of jeans
7 pairs of underwear	2 towels	1 washcloth
1 brush and comb	1 bottle of shampoo	1 bar of soap
1 bottle of sunscreen	1 bottle of insect spray	1 flashlight
1 toothbrush and tube of toothpaste	7 short-sleeve shirts	

There are many kinds of camps. There are church camps and scout camps. There are horseback-riding camps, swimming camps, music camps and nature camps. There are sports camps and cheerleading camps. There are even camps for losing weight!

Some city children take a bus to camp. The bus picks up a whole group of children and takes them to the country. Other children are taken to camp by their parents. Their parents look at their cabins. They sit on the bunk beds and say, "This feels comfortable." They look at the camp menu and say, "The food looks good." Then they say, "Good-bye. Have fun. Be careful. See you in a week!"

1. How many pairs of underwear do you need for a week at camp? __7__

2. How many pairs of shorts should you bring? __5__

3. How many things on the list do you need only one of? __11__

4. What are two things you could put your clothes in? __suitcase or gym bag__

5. Is there anything not listed that you think___ at camp? What?

6. If you we___ need to bring along?

Answers will vary.

73

Comprehension: Camping Out

Directions: Read about camping out. Then answer the questions.

Going away to camp and camping out are two very different experiences. Usually, children who go to camp sleep on cots inside cabins. Activities are planned by the people who run the camp. Campers eat in a dining hall. The food is prepared by someone else. All the campers have to do is show up and complain about what's being served!

When you camp out, the experience is much more rugged. You sleep in a tent instead of a cabin. If it's warm, you may unroll your sleeping bag under the stars. To camp out, you must be much more independent. You must learn certain skills, such as how to pitch a tent and how to start a fire. You need to know some rules about safety and respecting the outdoors. You may even need to know how to catch and cook your own food!

The Boy Scouts teach their members an "outdoor code" before they camp. It is a good code for any camper to follow. Here is a summary of the Boy Scouts' Outdoor Code:

"I will treat the outdoors as a heritage to be improved for greater enjoyment. I will keep my trash out of America's fields, woods and roadways. I will prevent wildfires. I will build my fire in a safe place and be sure it is out when I leave.

Use of the outdoors is a privilege I can lose by abuse. I will treat the environment with respect. I will learn to practice good conservation of soil, water, forests and wildlife, and I will urge others to do the same.

1. What are two of the things you need to know about before camping out?
__Answers may include: how to pitch a tent and start a fire__

2. What is the name of the camping rules the Boy Scouts are taught to follow?
__Boy Scouts' Outdoor Code__

3. What is one way Boy Scouts show they will treat the outdoors as a heritage to be improved?
__keep trash out of America's fields, woods and roadways/ prevent wildfires__

4. __Answers may include: sleep in tent, cook your own food, no planned activities__

74

Following Directions: Campfires

Directions: Read about building campfires. Then work the puzzle.

Where there is fire, there is always danger. That is why only people who know exactly what they are doing should build a campfire. Many campsites do not allow campfires. Campers bring portable cook stoves to these sites.

Sites that do allow campfires often provide firelays. A firelay is a 10-foot-round cleared area. In the area there may be a grill, metal ring or outdoor stone fireplace. These firelays are safe because they keep the fire contained in a small area. Firelays help keep cooking fires from spreading and turning into wildfires.

Across:
2. This is hot and always dangerous.
3. The shape of a firelay
4. When campfires are not allowed, use a _____ stove.
5. A _____ ring is sometimes found in a firelay.
7. Sometimes a _____ fireplace is provided in the firelay.

Down:
1. The purpose of a firelay is to make sure a fire doesn't _____.
2. 10-foot-round circles for building campfires
6. A firelay keeps the fire contained in a small _____.

Crossword answers:
- FIRE
- SPREAD
- ROUND
- PORTABLE
- METAL
- AREA
- STONE

Comprehension: First-Aid Kits

Directions: Read about first-aid kits. Then answer the questions.

Something you should be sure to take when you camp is a first-aid kit. Cuts, scrapes and insect bites or stings all can happen when camping. You must also be prepared for accidental poisoning. What if someone eats a berry that is poisonous? You will need to get the poison out of his/her system right away!

First-aid kits will help you in an emergency. Here are some things that go into a well-packed first-aid kit:

1 small bottle of ipecac syrup (Ipecac causes vomiting. It will immediately clear poison from the body.)
1 thermometer to check for fever
1 bottle of aspirin to hold down fever and ease pain
1 unopened bar of soap to wash cuts and scrapes
1 box of sterile bandages, adhesive tape and gauze pads for covering wounds after they have been cleaned
1 large triangular bandage to make a sling for an injured or broken arm
1 pair of tweezers to pull out splinters or bee stingers
1 bottle of calamine lotion to treat poison ivy and insect bites
1 bag of sterile cotton balls to clean cuts
1 eyecup and sterile water to wash out injured eyes

Many people keep first-aid kits in their cars. Then, if an emergency happens when they travel, they are always prepared. Does your family have a first-aid kit?

1. Why is a first-aid kit important when camping? **in case of an accident or poisoning**

2. What items in your first-aid kit would you use to treat these conditions?
A scrape? **soap, cotton balls, bandages**
A fever? **aspirin, thermometer**
A sprained arm? **triangular bandage**

3. When would you give someone ipecac syrup? **if they have eaten something poisonous**

Main Idea: Choosing a Campsite

Directions: Read about choosing a campsite. Then answer the questions.

If you are camping at a campground, you will not have much choice about where you camp. You must stay within the site area the owners show you. If you are camping in the wilderness, you can choose your own campsite.

A good campsite will have water nearby for drinking and cooking. Look for ground that is level and dry. Avoid rocky ground, or you will be uncomfortable when you try to sleep. If you plan to build a fire, look for dry firewood to gather nearby.

You will also need to be on the lookout for things you do not want. Hornets' nests, poison ivy and anthills can make your camping trip miserable. If you see any nearby, set up your campsite elsewhere. You will also want to avoid camping near bears or other animals. If you see animal tracks, take them as a sign that animals have already "staked out" the area. For your own safety, move on.

It's important when camping in the wilderness to let someone know where you are. Otherwise, if you get lost, no one will know! Then who would come to rescue you? Find the park rangers' station when you go into any wilderness area and talk to the rangers. It is their job to know the forest. They can tell you about which places to seek out and which to avoid.

A good plan is to promise to stop by after your trip. That way, they will know you returned safely. If you do not show up, they will come looking for you. Taking these few practical precautions will make your trip safer and more fun.

1. What is the main idea? (Check one.)

☑ Picking a good campsite and checking in with park rangers will help to make your wilderness camping trip a safe and enjoyable experience.

____ Avoiding poison ivy and anthills are the most important things you can do to make your wilderness trip a safe one.

____ Watch out for bears when you go camping.

2. Why should you tell park rangers where you will be? (Check one.)

____ They can bring messages to you if there is an emergency at home.

☑ They can send searchers to look for you if you do not return.

____ They can stop by for a cup of coffee if they get lonely.

Comprehension: Time to Eat!

Directions: Read about what to eat on a camping trip. Then answer the questions.

A wilderness camping trip will make you appreciate your kitchen, your bathroom, your bed and your comfortable living room furniture.

Food and water are among the most important things to bring on a camping trip. Remember, you will have to carry everything you need on your back. That's why it's smart to bring things that don't weigh too much. Because they are light, dried food and powdered drinks are good things for campers to bring. Then the campers add sterilized water to them and—presto!—a meal!

Many campers pack these foods: dry cereal, dried fruit, powdered eggs, raisins, dried potatoes, dried soup, powdered milk, instant cocoa, dried meat or dried chicken and rice. The total weight of all the food listed is under four pounds. Even a tired camper can carry four pounds easily. Imagine if you had to carry a gallon of milk, a couple of whole chickens, a roast, a bag of red potatoes and a dozen eggs! It would certainly weigh a lot more. Besides, the eggs would probably get broken, and the milk would get sour.

The best thing most people can say about dried food is that it's "not bad." If you have ever eaten it, you know that fresh, whole food tastes better. But the sights and sounds of camping in the wilderness make up for the dried food. If you are lucky, you will work up such an appetite hiking that even dried food will taste great!

1. Why do campers take along dried and powdered food? **because those things are light**

2. What is the best thing most people can say about dried food? **it's "not bad"**

3. What are five kinds of dried food? **Answers may include: cereal, fruit, potatoes, soup, meat, milk**

4. What is the total weight of all the dried food listed in the article? **4 pounds**

Recognizing Details: Three Kinds of Tents

Directions: Read about tents. Then answer the questions.

Tarp Tent
The tarp tent is the simplest tent. It is called a "one-man" tent because only one person will fit inside. Tarp tents have no floors. They have no windows or doors. They do not have netting. To put one up, you need to find a tree to hook one corner to.

Pup Tent
Two people can sleep in a pup tent. Some pup tents come with attached floors. They do not have windows. Like the tarp tent, the front of a pup tent is open. Pup tents have no doors.

Umbrella Tent
Umbrella tents are larger than pup tents or tarp tents. This means more people can sleep inside. They have floors and a door. Some have windows. The doors and windows can be left open. Netting can be pulled across the front of the doors and windows. The netting lets in air and keeps out bugs.

1. Which tents have no doors or windows? **tarp tent and pup tent**
2. Which tent needs to be pitched near a tree? **tarp tent**
3. Which tent has no floor? **tarp tent**
4. Which tent has netting to keep out bugs? **umbrella tent**
5. Which tent sleeps only one person? **tarp tent**
6. Which tent can two people sleep in? **pup tent**

Recognizing Details: Getting Lost

Directions: Read about what to do if you get lost in the woods. Then answer the questions.

Even experienced campers sometimes get lost. To avoid getting lost, stay on marked trails. Take a notepad and pencil with you for jotting notes. Use a compass so you know what direction you are going. To find your way with a compass, you must know which way you want to go. Before you leave your camp, find a large landmark nearby to mark your campsite. Head in the opposite direction from the landmark. If your compass shows you are going west, which direction will you travel to return to your campsite? East.

If you do get lost, don't panic. This is the worst thing you can do. People who panic have been known to walk in big circles. They don't realize this, of course. They exhaust themselves and never get back on course.

If it is late, and others know you are out hiking, stay where you are. Someone will come looking for you soon.

If it is early, and you want to try to find your way back, leave trail markers to show you where you have been. Tie a handkerchief to a branch. Put a pile of stones on the trail you have taken. If you have a pen and notepad in your pack, write a note and put it on a tree. Write down the time, date, the fact that you are lost and the direction you are now hiking.

If you are lost at night, build two campfires close together. Two columns of smoke side by side are a signal for help. Rangers and campers will recognize and respond to the fires. They will locate your smoke signals and come to find you.

In the meantime, use extra clothes from your pack to stay warm. Be patient and wait until help arrives.

1. Complete the directions on what to do if you get lost in the woods.
Tie a **handkerchief to a branch**
Put a pile **of stones on the trail you took**
If you have a pen and notepad, **write a note and put it on a tree**
If you are lost at night, build **two campfires**

2. What is the main idea? (Check one.)
____ It is nearly impossible to get lost while hiking.
____ If you get lost, use a compass to find your way back.
☑ Avoid panicking if you get lost by following some simple steps.

75   76   77   78   79   80

Review

Directions: Review what you learned about camping. Then answer the questions.

1. What items should you take on a camping trip? __Answers may include:__
__first aid kit, compass, dried food, tent, matches__

2. Of the items you wrote, circle the two you feel are the most __Answers will vary.__

3. Why is it important to carry camping gear and food that is light in weight?
__a heavy load makes you tired__

4. What should you look for when selecting a campsite? __Answers may include:__
__water nearby, level and dry ground, no signs of wild animals__

5. What would you not want near your site? __Hornets' nests, poison ivy,__
__anthills__

6. What are the safety reasons for finding a park rangers' station and talking to the rangers?
__They can tell you good places to camp, places to avoid__
__and search for you if you don't return.__

7. What can you do to avoid getting lost? __stay on marked trails, use a__
__compass__

8. What should you do if you do get lost? __stay calm, stay where you are__
__or leave trail markers to show where you have been__

9. Have you ever been camping? Explain your experience.

If not, describe what ~~Answers will vary.~~ to go camping.

81

Sequencing: "Mr. Nobody"

Directions: After reading the poem "Mr. Nobody," number in order the things people blame him for.

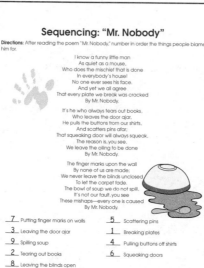

I know a funny little man
As quiet as a mouse,
Who does the mischief that is done
In everybody's house!
No one ever sees his face.
And yet we all agree
That every plate we break was cracked
By Mr. Nobody.

It's he who always tears out books,
Who leaves the door ajar,
He pulls the buttons from our shirts,
And scatters pins afar;
That squeaking door will always squeak,
The reason is, you see,
We leave the oiling to be done
By Mr. Nobody.

The finger marks upon the wall
By none of us are made;
We never leave the blinds unclosed
To let the carpet fade.
The bowl of soup we do not spill,
It's not our fault, you see
These mishaps—every one is caused
By Mr. Nobody.

__7__ Putting finger marks on walls

__3__ Leaving the door ajar

__9__ Spilling soup

__2__ Tearing out books

__8__ Leaving the blinds open

__5__ Scattering pins

__1__ Breaking plates

__4__ Pulling buttons off shirts

__6__ Squeaking doors

82

Comprehension: "The Chickens"

Directions: Read the poem "The Chickens." Then answer the questions.

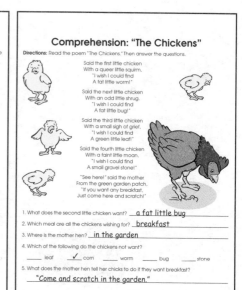

Said the first little chicken
With a queer little squirm,
"I wish I could find
A fat little worm!"

Said the next little chicken
With an odd little shrug,
"I wish I could find
A fat little bug!"

Said the third little chicken
With a small sigh of grief,
"I wish I could find
A green little leaf!"

Said the fourth little chicken
With a faint little moan,
"I wish I could find
A small gravel stone!"

"See here!" said the mother
From the green garden patch,
"If you want any breakfast,
Just come here and scratch!"

1. What does the second little chicken want? __a fat little bug__

2. Which meal are all the chickens wishing for? __breakfast__

3. Where is the mother hen? __in the garden__

4. Which of the following do the chickens not want?

____ leaf   _✓_ corn   ____ worm   ____ bug   ____ stone

5. What does the mother hen tell her chicks to do if they want breakfast?
__"Come and scratch in the garden."__

83

Following Directions: "I'm Glad"

Directions: Read the poem "I'm Glad." Then work the puzzle.

I'm glad the sky is painted blue
And the Earth is painted green,
With such a lot of nice fresh air
All sandwiched in between.

(crossword puzzle with answers: GREEN, BLUE, SANDWICHED, SKY, AIR, EARTH)

Across:
3. The sky is painted this color.
4. How what we breathe is placed between the Earth and sky.
6. This is what we breathe, and it's between the Earth and sky.

Down:
1. The color of the Earth in the poem
2. How the speaker feels
4. Painted blue
5. Painted green

84

Comprehension: "Over the Hills and Far Away"

Directions: Read "Over the Hills and Far Away." Then answer the questions.

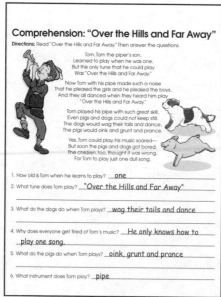

Tom, Tom the piper's son,
Learned to play when he was one,
But the only tune that he could play
Was "Over the Hills and Far Away."

Now Tom with his pipe made such a noise
That he pleased the girls and pleased the boys,
And they all danced when they heard him play
"Over the Hills and Far Away."

Tom played his pipe with such great skill,
Even pigs and dogs could not keep still.
The dogs would wag their tails and dance,
The pigs would oink and grunt and prance.

Yes, Tom could play, his music soared—
But soon the pigs and dogs got bored.
The children, too, thought it was wrong,
For Tom to play just one dull song.

1. How old is Tom when he learns to play? __one__

2. What tune does Tom play? __"Over the Hills and Far Away"__

3. What do the dogs do when Tom plays? __wag their tails and dance__

4. Why does everyone get tired of Tom's music? __He only knows how to__
__play one song.__

5. What do the pigs do when Tom plays? __oink, grunt and prance__

6. What instrument does Tom play? __pipe__

85

Sequencing: "The Spider and the Fly"

Directions: Read the poem "The Spider and the Fly." Then number the events in order.

"Won't you come into my parlor?" said the spider to the fly.
"It's the nicest little parlor that you will ever spy.
The way into my parlor is up a winding stair.
I have so many pretty things to show you inside there."

The little fly said, "No! No! No! To do so is not sane,
For those who travel up your stair do not come down again."

The spider turned himself around and went back in his den –
He knew for sure the silly fly would visit him again.
The spider wove a tiny web, for he was very sly
He was making preparations to trap the silly fly.

Then out his door the spider came and merrily did sing,
"Oh, fly, oh lovely, lovely fly with pearl and silver wings."

Alas! How quickly did the fly come buzzing back to hear
The spider's words of flattery, which drew the fly quite near.

The fly was trapped within the web, the spider's winding stair,
Then the spider jumped upon him, and ate the fly right there!

__4__ The spider sings a song about how beautiful the fly is.

__7__ The spider jumps on the fly.

__1__ The spider invites the fly into his parlor.

__3__ The spider spins a tiny new web to catch the fly.

__6__ The fly becomes caught in the spider's web.

__2__ The fly says he knows it's dangerous to go into the spider's parlor.

__8__ The spider eats the fly.

__5__ The fly comes near the web to hear the song.

86

Comprehension: "Grasshopper Green"

Directions: Read the poem "Grasshopper Green." Then answer the questions.

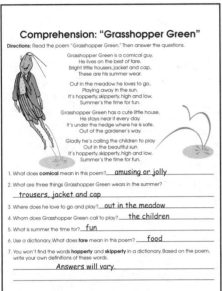

Grasshopper Green is a comical guy.
He lives on the best of fare.
Bright little trousers, jacket and cap,
These are his summer wear.

Out in the meadow he loves to go,
Playing away in the sun.
It's hopperty, skipperty, high and low,
Summer's the time for fun.

Grasshopper Green has a cute little house,
He stays near it every day.
It's under the hedge where he is safe,
Out of the gardener's way.

Gladly he's calling the children to play,
Out in the beautiful sun
It's hopperty, skipperty, high and low,
Summer's the time for fun.

1. What does **comical** mean in this poem? __amusing or jolly__

2. What are three things Grasshopper Green wears in the summer?
__trousers, jacket and cap__

3. Where does he love to go and play? __out in the meadow__

4. Whom does Grasshopper Green call to play? __the children__

5. What is summer the time for? __fun__

6. Use a dictionary. What does **fare** mean in this poem? __food__

7. You won't find the words **hopperty** and **skipperty** in a dictionary. Based on the poem, write your own definitions of these words.
__Answers will vary.__

87

Main Idea: "Little Robin Redbreast"

Directions: Read the poem "Little Robin Redbreast." Then answer the questions.

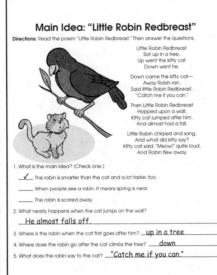

Little Robin Redbreast
Sat up in a tree,
Up went the kitty cat
Down went he.

Down came the kitty cat—
Away Robin ran,
Said little Robin Redbreast,
"Catch me if you can."

Then Little Robin Redbreast
Hopped upon a wall,
Kitty cat jumped after him,
And almost had a fall.

Little Robin chirped and sang,
And what did kitty say?
Kitty cat said, "Meow!" quite loud,
And Robin flew away.

1. What is the main idea? (Check one.)

✓ The robin is smarter than the cat and a lot faster, too.

____ When people see a robin, it means spring is near.

____ The robin is scared away.

2. What nearly happens when the cat jumps on the wall?
__He almost falls off.__

3. Where is the robin when the cat first goes after him? __up in a tree__

4. Where does the robin go after the cat climbs the tree? __down__

5. What does the robin say to the cat? __"Catch me if you can."__

88

Sequencing: "Hickory, Dickory, Dock"

Directions: Read the poem "Hickory, Dickory, Dock." Then answer the questions.

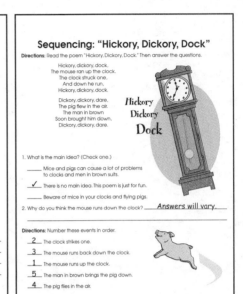

Hickory, dickory, dock.
The mouse ran up the clock.
The clock struck one,
And down he run,
Hickory, dickory, dock.

Dickory, dickory, dare.
The pig flew in the air.
The man in brown
Soon brought him down,
Dickory, dickory, dare.

Hickory Dickory Dock

1. What is the main idea? (Check one.)

____ Mice and pigs can cause a lot of problems to clocks and men in brown suits.

✓ There is no main idea. This poem is just for fun.

____ Beware of mice in your clocks and flying pigs.

2. Why do you think the mouse runs down the clock? __Answers will vary.__

Directions: Number these events in order.

_2_ The clock strikes one.

_3_ The mouse runs back down the clock.

_1_ The mouse runs up the clock.

_5_ The man in brown brings the pig down.

_4_ The pig flies in the air.

89

Review

Directions: Review the poems you read. Then answer the questions.

1. How is the spider in the poem "The Spider and the Fly" like the fox in the fable "The Fox and the Crow"?
__Answers may include: Both the spider and the fox use__
__flattery to trick someone.__

2. Which of the poems that you read did you like the best?
Why?

3. Which of the poems that you _____
Why?

Answers will vary.

One way to remember what you read is to make a comic strip of the story or poem. Think about the poem "Mr. Nobody." Imagine what "Mr. Nobody" would look like.

Directions: Follow the sequence of events in the "Mr. Nobody" poem to make a cartoon of the poem in the boxes below

Cartoons will vary.

90

Review

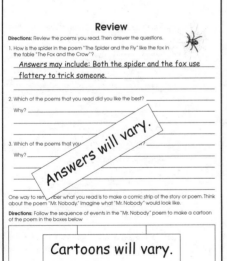

Directions: Select one of the other poems you read. Summarize and illustrate it.

Pictures will vary.

91

Recognizing Details: Earth's Atmosphere

Directions: Read about Earth's atmosphere. Then answer the questions.

The air that surrounds Earth is called the atmosphere. It surrounds Earth like a blanket—20 miles thick! The atmosphere protects Earth from the sun's heat. It helps keep heat in, too. If we had no atmosphere, the sun would fry Earth during the day. At night, it would be freezing! Earth's heat would escape into outer space. Nothing could stay alive on Earth without the atmosphere to protect us.

Did you know air can be weighed? If we could weigh the air in our atmosphere, it would weigh 6,000,000,000,000,000 (or six quadrillion) pounds. This huge figure is based on what scientists have figured out.

The air in the atmosphere is made up of dust and gases. More than three-fourths of the gas is nitrogen. Plants depend on nitrogen to stay alive. Most of the rest is made up of oxygen. Oxygen is needed for human and animal life. One percent of the atmosphere is made up of other gases. Included in this one percent are dust particles, ash from volcanoes and other bits of matter.

The gases and particles in the atmosphere are packed closer together near the ground. The farther up you go, the farther apart the gases and particles are. People who travel to the mountains find it harder to breathe the air. This is because the air is "thinner" and their lungs are not used to it. They have to work a little harder to get oxygen from this thin air. Usually, their lungs adjust quickly.

1. What are two ways the atmosphere protects Earth? __It keeps the Earth__
__from getting too hot during the day and too cold during__
__the night.__

2. What gas makes up most of the atmosphere? __nitrogen__

3. Where are gases and particles in the atmosphere packed closest together?
__near the ground__

4. Why is it harder to breathe in the mountains? __the air is thinner__

5. How thick is the atmosphere? __20 miles__

92

Comprehension: Earth's Atmosphere

Directions: Review what you read about Earth's atmosphere. Then answer the questions.

1. To what does the article compare the atmosphere? __a blanket__

2. Why is air in our atmosphere so important? __It is made up of gases like nitrogen and oxygen which plants and animals need to live.__

3. How do you think thinner air in the mountains aff__ ___ __and animal life?__

4. What do you think would happen __ ___ ___ ___ heat would reach Earth?__

5. What do you think would __ ___ ___ the Sun's heat did not remain trapped close to Earth at night?__

Answers will vary.

Scientists know that __ ___ ___here is continuing to thin, thus losing its ability to protect Earth from the sun's u__ __olet rays.

Directions: Use reference sources to find out more about Earth's thinning atmosphere. Select one of the topics and write a report based on your research. Include illustrations or diagrams if possible.

What is the ozone layer?
What is the Greenhouse Effect?
What caused the hole in the ozone?
What is being done about the hole in the ozone?
What is being done about the Greenhouse Effect?
What will happen if the hole in the ozone gets larger?
What will happen if the Greenhouse Effect continues?

93

Comprehension: Clouds

Directions: Read about clouds. Then answer the questions.

Have you ever wondered where clouds come from? Clouds are made from billions and billions of tiny water droplets in the air. The water droplets form into clouds when warm, moist air rises and is cooled.

Have you ever seen your breath when you were outside on a very cold day? Your breath is warm and moist. When it hits the cold air, it is cooled. A kind of small cloud is formed by your breath!

Clouds come in many sizes and shapes. On some days, clouds blanket the whole sky. Other times, clouds look like wispy puffs of smoke. There are other types of clouds as well.

Weather experts have named clouds. Big, fluffy clouds that look flat on the bottom are called **cumulus** clouds. **Strato-cumulus** is the name for rounded clouds that are packed very close together. You can still see patches of sky, but strato-cumulus clouds are thicker than cumulus ones.

If you spot **cumulo-nimbus** clouds, go inside. These clouds are wide at the bottom and have thin tops. The tops of these clouds are filled with ice crystals. On hot summer days, you may even have seen cumulo-nimbus clouds growing. They seem to boil and grow as though they are coming from a big pot. A violent thunderstorm usually occurs after you see these clouds. Often, there is hail.

Cumulus, strato-cumulus and cumulo-nimbus are only three of many types of clouds. If you listen closely, you will hear television weather forecasters talk about these and other clouds. Why? Because clouds are good indicators of weather.

1. How are clouds formed? __Water droplets in the air form clouds when warm, moist air rises and cools.__

2. How can you make your own cloud? __by breathing outside on a cold day__

3. What should you do when you spot cumulo-nimbus clouds? __go inside__

4. What often happens after you see cumulo-nimbus clouds? __violent thunderstorms, sometimes hail__

5. What kind of big fluffy clouds look flat on the bottom? __cumulus__

94

Recognizing Details: Clouds

Directions: Review what you learned about clouds. Then answer the questions.

1. How are clouds a good indicator of the weather? __Some types of clouds can bring rain, snow or hail.__

2. When you take something out of the freezer on a warm day, why do you think it looks like steam is rising from the object? __Answers will vary.__

3. What does this have to do with clouds? __Clouds are formed in the same way.__

Directions: Use cotton balls to make models of the three types of clouds.

95

Following Directions: Rain

Directions: Read about rain. Then work the puzzle.

Rain develops from water vapor, dust and temperature inside clouds. From this combination, water droplets form and grow. When the droplets become too heavy for the cloud, they fall as rain. Weather experts say that when it storms, the raindrops are about 0.02 inches (0.5 millimeters) in size.

Sometimes the air below the rain cloud is very dry. The dry air dries out the wetness of the raindrop and turns it back into water vapor before it hits the ground. This is what happens in the summer when it looks as though it will rain but doesn't. The rain begins to fall, but it dries up before it falls all the way to the ground.

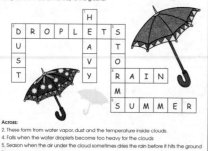

Crossword puzzle:
- D R O P L E T S
- U / A / H
- S / V / O
- T / Y / R A I N
- M
- S U M M E R

Across:
2. These form from water vapor, dust and the temperature inside clouds.
4. Falls when the water droplets become too heavy for the clouds
5. Season when the air under the cloud sometimes dries the rain before it hits the ground

Down:
1. When water droplets inside clouds get this way, rain falls.
2. Combines with water vapor and the temperature inside clouds.
3. Raindrops measure about 0.02 inches (0.5 mm) when it _____.

96

Comprehension: Thunderstorms

Directions: Read about thunderstorms. Then answer the questions.

Thunderstorms can be scary! The sky darkens. The air feels heavy. Then the thunder begins. Sometimes the thunder sounds like a low rumble. Other times thunder is very loud. Loud thunder can be heard 15 miles away.

Thunderstorms begin inside big cumulo-nimbus clouds. Remember, cumulo-nimbus are the summer clouds that seem to boil and grow. It is as though there is a big pot under the clouds.

Thunder is heard after lightning flashes across the sky. The noise of thunder happens when lightning heats the air as it cuts through it. Some people call this quick, sharp sound a thunderclap. Other times thunder sounds "rumbly." This rumble is the thunder's sound wave bouncing off hills and mountains.

Weather experts say there is an easy way to figure out how far away a storm is. First, look at your watch. Count the number of seconds between the flash of lightning and the sound of thunder. To find how far away the storm is, divide the number of seconds by five. This will give the number of miles the storm is from you.

How far away is the storm if you count 20 seconds between the flash of lightning and the sound of thunder? Twenty divided by five is four miles. What if you count only five seconds? One mile! Get inside quickly. The air is charged with electricity. You could be stuck by lightning. It is not safe to be outside in a thunderstorm.

1. Where do thunderstorms begin? __inside cumulo-nimbus clouds__

2. When is thunder heard? __after lightning flashes__

3. What causes thunder to sound rumbly? __the sound wave bounces off hills and mountains__

4. To find out how far away a storm is, count the seconds between the thunder and lightning and divide by what number? __5__

5. If you count 40 seconds between the lightning and thunder, how far away is the storm? __8 miles__

6. What comes first, thunder or lightning? __lightning__

97

Recognizing Details: Lightning Safety

Directions: Read about safety rules for lightning. Then answer the questions.

During a storm, lightning can be very dangerous. If you are outside when a thunderstorm begins, look for shelter in a building. If you are in the woods, look for a cave. If you are in an open field, lie down in a hole. If there is no hole, lie flat on the ground.

Standing in an open field, your body is like a lightning rod. Never look for shelter under a tree during a thunderstorm. Lightning is even more likely to strike there! You and the tree are two lightning rods standing together.

Water is also a good conductor of electricity. You must never go into the water when a storm is brewing. The air becomes charged. The charge attracts lightning. The lightning has to go somewhere, and it may go into the water. That is why lifeguards order everyone out of the pool even before a storm comes.

If a thunderstorm comes up when you are boating, get to shore fast. Do not hold fishing rods or other metal objects. They attract lightning.

A car is a good, safe place to be in a thunderstorm. The rubber tires "ground" the car's metal body and remove its charge. This means the electricity cannot go through the car. Lightning does not strike cars. You are safe inside a car.

1. What should you do if you are in a field when a thunderstorm begins? __lie down in a hole or flat on the ground__

2. What is your body like if you are outside during a thunderstorm? __a lightning rod__

3. Why do lifeguards order people from the pool before a thunderstorm? __Water is a good conductor of electricity.__

4. Where is a good place to be during a thunderstorm? __in a car or a building__

5. Besides the human body, name two things that attract lightning. __Answers may include: trees, water, metal objects__

98

Review

Directions: Review what you learned about rain, thunder and lightning. Then answer the questions.

1. How are thunderstorms different from rain showers? _____
   Thunderstorms include lightning, thunder, strong winds and sometimes hail.

2. Do you think thunderstorms are scary? Explain. Answers will vary.

3. What is thunder? The noise made when lightning heats the air as it cuts through it.

4. Why do you think some thunder is louder or softer than other thunder? because it's closer (louder) or farther away (softer)

5. Why shouldn't you be outside in a storm? You could be struck by lightning

6. Name ways you can seek shelter during a storm if you are:
   outside: in a building
   in the woods: in a cave
   in a field: in a hole or ditch
   in a field with no hole: lie down flat on the ground

7. What makes a car a safe place during a storm? The rubber tires "ground" the cars body and removes its charge.

8. Would you have thought this to be true? Why or why not? Answers will vary.

99

Comprehension: Hurricanes

Directions: Read about hurricanes. Then answer the questions.

Have you ever been in a hurricane? If you are lucky, you have not. Hurricanes are deadly! Thunderstorms are scary and can cause damage, but hurricanes are the most destructive storms on Earth.

There are three "ingredients" in a hurricane. They are turbulent oceans, fierce winds and lashing rains. Hurricane winds can blow as fast as 180 miles (290 kilometers) an hour. They can pull up trees, buildings, cars and people. Hurricanes can destroy anything in their paths.

There are other names for hurricanes. In some parts of the world, they are called cyclones. The people who live on the islands in the Pacific Ocean call them typhoons. In Australia, some people use a funny name to describe these terrible storms. They call them "willy-willies."

Although hurricanes can occur in most parts of the world, they all start in the same place. The place hurricanes are "born" is over the ocean near the equator.

Here is how a hurricane is born. At the equator, the sun is very, very hot. The scorching sun beats down on the ocean water. It heats the water and the air above the water. The heated air begins to spiral upward in tiny, hot circles. When the heated air combines with moist air, it is drawn farther up toward the sky.

The spiral of heated air and moist air begins to twist. As it twists, it grows. As it grows, it spins faster and faster in a counterclockwise direction. (This means in the opposite direction from the way a clock's hands move.) Huge rain clouds form at the top of the spiral as the air at the top is cooled. The combination of rain, hot air and spiraling winds creates a hurricane.

1. What are other names for hurricanes? cyclones, typhoons, willy-willies

2. Where do all hurricanes begin? over the ocean near the equator

3. What direction does a hurricane's spiral move? counterclockwise

4. What three "ingredients" are needed to produce a hurricane? turbulent oceans, fierce winds and lashing rain

100

Recognizing Details: Hurricanes

Directions: Review what you learned about hurricanes. Then answer the questions.

1. What is the most destructive type of storm on Earth? a hurricane

2. What makes them so destructive? The high winds can pull up trees, buildings, people and cars.

3. What makes hurricanes scarier than thunderstorms? Hurricanes are more destructive.

4. How do hurricanes form? The sun heats the ocean surface and the air above it, the hot air rises in spirals, then the hot air combines with moist air and begins to twist and grow.

5. What parts of the United States are most likely to be struck by a hurricane? areas in the southern United States along the coast of the ocean

6. Many people enjoy living or vacationing in beach areas. Do you think they would feel the same way if they were on the coast when a hurricane happened? Explain. Answers will vary.

7. What does counterclockwise mean? in the opposite direction from the way a clock's hands move

101

Main Idea: Tornadoes

Directions: Read about tornadoes. Then answer the questions.

Another type of dangerous weather condition is a tornado. While hurricanes form over water, tornadoes form over land. Tornadoes are more likely to form in some locations than in others. The areas where tornadoes frequently form are called "tornado belts." In the United States, a major tornado belt is the basin of land between Missouri and Mississippi.

Tornadoes are formed when masses of hot air meet masses of cold air. When these air masses slam together, bad thunderstorms begin. People in tornado belts are fearful when a severe storm threatens. They know a tornado may occur if the warm, moist air rushes upward and begins to spiral.

The tornado forms a funnel cloud. The funnel is narrow at the base and broad at the top. The tornado's funnel cloud can move very fast. The winds around the funnel can move 300 miles an hour. The winds inside the funnel are fast, too. The tornado acts like a giant vacuum cleaner. It sucks up everything in its path. People, animals, cars and houses are all in danger when a tornado strikes.

It is difficult to stay out of a tornado's path. The way it moves is unpredictable. It may move straight or in a zig-zag pattern. The winds of the tornado make a screaming noise like a huge train rushing by. People who have lived through a tornado usually say it was the most frightening experience of their lives.

1. What is the main idea? (Check one.)

   ____ Tornadoes form over land and hurricanes form over water.

   ____ Tornados sound like a rushing train.

   ✓ Tornadoes, which form over land under certain weather conditions, are dangerous and frightening.

2. How fast can the winds around the funnel cloud move? 300 miles per hour

3. Why is it hard to stay out of the path of a tornado? the path is unpredictable

4. What household appliance can a tornado be compared to? vacuum cleaner

102

Recognizing Details: Tornadoes

Directions: Review what you learned about tornadoes. Then answer the questions.

1. How do tornadoes form? Tornadoes form when masses of warm air meet masses of cold air.

2. What shape is a tornado? a funnel

3. What makes a tornado so dangerous? high winds and an unpredictable path

4. Which type of storm do you think is more dangerous, a tornado or a hurricane? Why? Answers will vary.

5. What types of weather conditions are not dangerous? Answers may include rain or snow showers.

6. What types of winter storms are also dangerous? Why? Answers may include: blizzards, ice storms

Directions: Compare and contrast tornadoes and hurricanes in the Venn diagram.

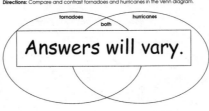

tornadoes   hurricanes
both

Answers will vary.

103

Review

Directions: Read this Native American legend about Lightning. Then answer the questions.

In the beginning, Lightning lived on Earth among people. Soon, he became so powerful that people were afraid. He lashed out and killed some of them. The people grew to hate him.

After Lightning had killed many people, the chiefs of the tribes got together. They had to decide what to do about Lightning. They agreed to tell Lightning he could no longer live on Earth. He begged to stay, but the chiefs forced him to leave.

Shortly after Lightning left, a great monster began to carry people away. The monster lived deep underground. The people could not kill the monster. He always escaped underground before they could catch him.

Lightning heard about their trouble. He came back to the chiefs. "I will kill the monster," he told them. "But in return, you must let me live among you again."

Because he was the only one who could kill the great monster, the chiefs let Lightning return. He did not change his ways much. He is still dangerous. To this day, that is why we have Lightning on Earth.

1. What is the main idea? (Check one.)

_____ Lightning was mean and killed many people, so the chiefs sent him away.

__✓__ The chiefs sent Lightning away because he was mean, but they agreed to let him return to save them from the great monster.

_____ There are worse things than Lightning.

2. Why couldn't the people kill the great monster themselves? _____
   He escaped underground before they could catch him.

3. Why did the chiefs agree to let Lightning return to Earth? __Lightning was__
   the only one who could kill the great monster.

104

Review

Directions: Write your own Native American legend about Tornado or Hurricane.

Legends will vary.

105

Teaching Suggestions

Comprehension

Comprehension involves understanding what is seen, heard or read. To help your child with this skill, talk about a book, movie or television program you've enjoyed together. Ask your child what it was about and if he/she liked it. If your child comprehends what he/she has seen or read, he/she should be able to recount the main events in sequential order and retell the story in his/her own words.

By listening to what he/she says, you can tell whether the book, movie, etc. was understood. If your child does not fully understand part of it, discuss that section further. Reread the book or watch the program again, if possible.

Your child can make an advertising poster for a book or movie. Have him/her include the important events, most exciting parts, favorite part and reasons why someone else should read or view it.

Creating a book jacket for a book he/she has read is another way for your child to show he/she has understood what was read. The jacket should include a picture depicting a main event in the story and a brief summary on the back. If the book belongs to your child, he/she could use the cover on the book.

Main Idea

Newspapers are one of the most convenient and versatile learning tools you have around your home. Encourage your child to read parts of the newspaper every day.

You might notice a headline that looks interesting and ask your child to read the article and tell you what it is about. This helps him/her find the main idea of an article.

Look for articles of interest to your child—ones about neighborhood events, people you know, items relating to school and special hobbies or sports of interest to your child. Sometimes it helps to cut out articles and let your child read one article a day. It can be less intimidating to start by reading one short article than to try to read an entire newspaper.

Leave your newspaper folded in such a way that an interesting photo or headline is showing. That may help catch your child's attention and encourage him/her to read that article and others.

When an interesting story is developing in your local newspaper, encourage your child to follow it for several days to learn the latest developments. Have him/her select the main idea of the story and write it down each day. After several days, he/she will have a sequential report of the story.

Encourage your child to read editorials and write an editorial to the paper expressing his/her views.

Following Directions

Let your child help with the cooking and baking. Not only does this give your child good experience in reading and following directions, he/she also uses many math skills to measure ingredients. Have your child look for recipes in newspapers and magazines, as well as cookbooks. Most libraries have a large selection of cookbooks. It's a fun way to learn, and the results can be delicious.

Cooking is one of many daily activities that involves following directions. Whether it is heating a can of vegetables, cooking a frozen pizza or making pudding, all involve following directions. Read the package directions with your child and have him/her help you.

Ask your child to take a turn preparing a meal for the family once a week. Write out the directions and be very specific. Remember, until he/she has had experience cooking, what seems obvious to you may not be obvious to your child. For example, if you tell your child to add a can of vegetables to make a casserole and don't mention that the vegetables should be drained first, you might end up with a very juicy casserole.

When you have a bicycle, toy, or other item to assemble, allow your child to help. Point to each step in the directions. Read each step together. Then follow the steps in order. Like following package directions or a recipe, assembling an item enables your child to see that following directions is a skill used in everyday situations.

Building models and making craft projects are other ways for your child to learn to follow directions. Reading the instructions and learning to play a new board game or video game helps your child practice this skill.

Recognizing Details

It is important for your child to be able to recognize and remember details of what he/she has read and seen. After reading a book or watching a movie together, ask your child questions about details, like what the main character wore, when and where the story took place, names of minor characters, etc.

Encourage your child to be observant about details in everyday life. After walking or driving past a building or billboard, ask your child to recall as many details as possible.

Play a game to help strengthen your child's attention to detail. Gather 20 to 25 common everyday objects and set them out on a table (button, dice, pen, scissors, cup, spoon, small toys, book, paper clip, straw, spool of thread, disk, etc.). Ask your child to study the objects and see how many he/she can remember. Then cover the objects with a towel and ask him/her to name as many as possible. Do this several times with the same items, then with a different set of items.

Sequencing

Sequencing can be done in several ways. Words can be arranged in alphabetical order. Events can be arranged in chronological order. Steps to complete a task can be arranged in logical order. Items can be arranged by size or shape from largest to smallest.

Present a math word problem for your child to solve. Have him/her explain and write in sequence how to solve the problem.

As you are traveling, tell a story together. Begin the story. After a few sentences, have your child continue the story. Take turns until you arrive at your destination or get to the end of the story.

Find a comic strip that has three or four sections and read it with your child. Cut the sections apart and have your child put them back together.

Encourage your child to tell you about events that have occurred at school or other places where you were not present. As he/she recalls what happened, encourage him/her to recall the events in order and add details.

Have your child keep a journal. This not only helps with sequencing but is also a good way to record what is happening in his/her life for the future. Each night in the journal, have your child write in order four things that he/she did during the day. When the journal is full, put it away in a safe place and save it for your child to reread when he/she is a few years older.

Fables and Legends

Read fables and legends from many cultures with your child. Check your library or favorite bookstore for titles. After reading several together, make up your own. Brainstorm some ideas and write them down in the form of a question: Why is the sky blue? Why do birds fly? How did a giraffe get such a long neck? Why are hummingbirds so small? Select one and make up your story together. You can write it or tape it, then read or play it back. Encourage your child to draw an illustration for your legend or fable.

Poetry

Read poems you enjoyed as a child together with your own child. Ask your child to share his/her favorite poems with you.

Libraries carry many good anthologies of poetry, from nursery rhymes to long, narrative poems. Sample many different kinds including both rhymed and unrhymed verse. Limericks are always fun to read and write. If your child says he/she doesn't like poetry, try authors like Ogden Nash and Edward Lear.